Emerging
markets

Founded in 1807, John Wiley & Sons is the oldest independent publishing company in the United States. With offices in North America, Europe, Australia and Asia, Wiley is globally committed to developing and marketing print and electronic products and services for our customers' professional and personal knowledge and understanding.

The Wiley Finance series contains books written specifically for finance and investment professionals as well as sophisticated individual investors and their financial advisors. Book topics range from portfolio management to e-commerce, risk management, financial engineering, valuation and financial instrument analysis, as well as much more.

For a list of available titles, please visit our Web site at www.WileyFinance.com

Emerging markets

A Practical Guide for Corporations, Lenders, and Investors

JEFFREY C. HOOKE

John Wiley & Sons, Inc.

New York • Chichester • Weinheim • Brisbane • Singapore • Toronto

This title is also available in print as ISBN 0-471-36099-6

For more information about Wiley products, visit our web site at www.Wiley.com

preface

In 1991, after a 10-year career in U.S. investment banking, I began doing deals in the developing world. My first stop was the International Finance Corporation, the World Bank's $8 billion private sector affiliate, which was then the largest direct investor in these growing economies. My assignment was to investigate and close large transactions in Latin America. I was struck by the seeming diversity of the business climates, but as time passed, patterns became evident. Unscientifically, perhaps, I initially concluded the similarities stemmed from the common Spanish heritage. Little did I know that such patterns crossed national borders and continents.

In 1998, I jumped to the $1.8 billion AIG-Asian Infrastructure Fund, the largest private equity partnership devoted to the emerging markets. Here, I arranged sizeable equity financings in Asia. After doing business in China, Thailand, and South Korea, I observed that my Asian transactions—at least from a Western perspective—shared issues that were strikingly similar to my Latin deals. Following the successes and disappointments of these experiences, I realized that I had learned many lessons that deserved closer study. These lessons could also benefit others. Hence, this book.

Government deregulation and privatization in these countries—combined with the globalization trend and a U.S. economic slowdown—stimulated investor interest in the early 1990s and tens of billions of dollars flowed to these economies. This enthusiasm produced mind-boggling returns for the early entrants, but later players saw their performance tempered by the Tequila effect (1995), the Asian crisis (1997), and the Russian default (1998). These setbacks produced a hangover from which these markets have yet to recover.

Compared to the 1990s, Westerners are now more careful before making a commitment, since they've seen what happens when a developing economy hits bottom.

Bent, perhaps, but not broken, the emerging market investment story contains the seeds of optimism, yet it is no fairy tale. The economies remain volatile and the business environment is difficult for those Western corporations, lenders, and investors who enter less than fully prepared.

Although the pronoun "he" has been used throughout this book to refer to corporate executives and investors, the material herein will be equally useful to both men and women who are evaluating emerging markets investments.

In addition to my own activities, *Emerging Markets* reflects the experiences of dozens of executives active in Latin America, Asia, Eastern Europe, and Africa. Exchanges with them took place in airports, business meetings, conferences, luncheon conversations, and formal interviews and most of the quotes in the book derive from these discussions. For the most part, the themes relate best to Western investors seeking to make long-term commitments as opposed to import/export arrangements, and the book provides a solid foundation from which to build the requisite decision-making process. Its approach is practical and well-balanced, enabling you to size-up the opportunities and pitfalls ahead.

JEFFREY C. HOOKE

Chevy Chase, Maryland
April 2001

acknowledgements

I want to thank the many people who took time out of their busy schedules to talk with me about the emerging markets. A special thanks to the staff at John Wiley & Sons: Bill Falloon, Mary Daniello, and Jennifer MacDonald. Nancy Marcus Land of Publications Development Company was of great assistance. Bruce Gouldey, Andy Klingenstein, Steve Ritterbush, and Angie Klint at Fairfax Partners deserve my thanks, as well as Barbara Hooke and Rosario Caceres. I also appreciate the understanding of my wife, Patty, and my two sons, Matt and Greg, during the writing of this book.

J.C.H.

contents

Emerging
markets

CHAPTER 1

Introduction

Money and business have gone global, so it's important for an executive to have an international perspective. A growing part of the world economy is represented by the emerging markets (see Figure 1.1)—a collection of 156 poor countries in various stages of development. Accounting for 84 percent of the world's population and 76 percent of its land mass, they are an important adjunct to the dominant economies of the United States, Japan, and Western Europe, and they attract considerable interest from multinational corporations, investors, and financial institutions. However, Westernized participants must be cognizant of the unique business environment that emerging markets signify. Developing countries are extremely diverse in language, politics, and culture, yet patterns of business behavior and circumstance are recognizable. The purpose of this book is to educate the reader about these commonalities and provide prospective investors with a foundation that supports a practical decision-making process.

UNEVEN PLAYING FIELDS

Emerging markets are difficult places for Westerners to do business. Besides the myriad risks associated with any economic venture, the foreign corporation or financial institution seeking to operate in these markets walks into a tough game. Investments and imports from wealthy countries are subject to special restrictions, taxes, and

FIGURE 1.1 Emerging markets cover the globe with the exception of the United States, Canada, Western Europe, Greece, Israel, Kuwait, U.A.E., Japan, Taiwan, Singapore, Australia, and New Zealand—all shown with a large star.

red tape that preserve local oligopolies and limit foreigners' profits. This makes a "joint" venture with a local partner—who knows the right buttons to push and the right officials to groom—de rigueur. Even then, the outsider must pay close attention to what's going on, lest additional impediments interfere with the profit objective.

My experience collecting on a defaulted loan is illustrative. In 1988, the International Finance Corporation (IFC) invested $13 million in a Mexican pulp mill, of which $10 million was a loan and $3 million was in common stock. The controlling stockholder in the business was Grupo Industrial Durango, S.A. (GID), a regional concern that conducted a sizeable paper and packaging business. By 1991, pulp prices had plummeted, rendering the project uneconomic, and Celulosa y Papel de Durango, S.A. (Celpap) stopped payments on the loan. Pursuant to a support agreement, GID was required to "backstop" the loan, but it backed away from the obligation, citing a technicality in the legal documents.

In the United States, a commercial lender in a similar position would have accelerated the loan, taken control of the project, sold the assets, and sued GID for whatever losses occurred. However, the sponsor's support obligation was under local jurisdiction. Under Mexican law, the process of foreclosure takes 6 to 12 months, and the mechanics of a subsequent liquidation require years. Furthermore, Mexican jurisprudence had few precedents in the interpretation of debt support agreements, and the IFC feared a local judge would simply void the entire arrangement, even though similar supports were widely accepted elsewhere.

As part of the influential World Bank (which includes Mexico as both shareholder and borrower), the IFC should have been immune to legal discrimination in a backwater town like Durango, but my superiors refused to stake the IFC's political capital on a $10 million investment. If an agent of the World Bank can't get a fair hearing in Mexican courts, I wondered, how are multinationals going to fare?

The IFC had been in on-again, off-again negotiations with GID for several years. When IFC's foreclosure threats rang hollow,

GID realized it was in the driver's seat, and offered few concessions. IFC decided a new face might move things along, and I was asked because of my ability to negotiate in a variety of situations. This businessman's first impression of the dusty mining town of Durango was full of surprises. The town was located in the Sonoran desert and, as I learned later, the area's dry, stark scenery made it a popular filming location for old cowboy movies. But what a strange place to put a pulp mill! Shouldn't it have situated in a wetter climate, with forests and trees? Later, in a moment of candor, one GID official told me the federal government, through misguided policies and pork-barrel politics, pushed jobs to Durango by building a $200 million paper plant nearby. This white elephant was the pulp mill's only customer.

Situated in an area lacking forests and water supplies (paper factories use a lot of water), the facility operated at a loss for years. Eventually, the Mexican government privatized the plant in one of its suspicious auctions, and GID bought the assets for pennies on the dollar. Substituting waste paper as the principal raw material instead of pulp, GID put the facility into the black, but in doing so, the pulp mill lost its customer.

When I arrived at GID's headquarters, information that we had requested weeks before was unavailable or missing, and GID's executives assigned to the negotiations forgot how to speak English, complicating matters and forcing me to translate for IFC's technical expert. During a tour of the pulp mill, we noticed that key pieces of equipment were missing. Since the equipment weighed several tons, we concluded that GID removed it to raise cash, obviously in violation of the loan agreement.

Negotiations went nowhere, and I returned to Washington, convinced that the IFC had a total loss on its hands. A few weeks later I met a Chase Manhattan banker at a hotel in Monterrey, Mexico. The bank had syndicated two large loans for GID, and he let slip that the company was filing for a $200 million initial public offering (IPO) on the New York Stock Exchange. After some detective work, I discovered that Morgan Stanley & Co., the white-shoe investment banking firm, was leading the IPO. The fact that GID, a marginal operation at best, attracted top-tier financiers, like Chase Manhattan and Morgan Stanley, puzzled me, but when investors are hungry for emerging market paper, I suppose it's the banks' job to feed them.

My calls to the Morgan Stanley executive leading the transaction went unanswered, and the IPO filing moved through the regulatory process of the Securities and Exchange Commission. When I finally connected, this executive gave me the brush off, and shortly thereafter, the company started its "road show." My leverage was strongest when GID had no recourse, so I waited until U.S. institutional investors had reviewed the deal. At the last hour, I notified the company and Morgan Stanley, in writing, that the IPO prospectus didn't include a description of the IFC dispute and the resultant potential for litigation. Knowing that few institutions would put money into a company that had welched on a World Bank obligation, GID sent a $6 million settlement package across my desk two days later.

The IFC made a partial recovery of its joint venture investment, but the average foreign investor faces rough treatment when things go wrong. Emerging markets lack the legal infrastructure for workout situations, and courts lean heavily toward local interests. Financial regulators and local legislatures show little inclination toward leveling the playing field for outsiders.

UNREALISTIC TERMS

This cold reality clashes with the developing nations' stated desire for foreign investments, which can bring jobs and progress. The countries want outside monies, but only on their own terms, which are usually unrealistic from the Western point of view. For example, after the spectacular economic crashes in Asia, the local business owners were often broke, yet they refused to sell out to cash-rich multinationals. Their asking prices prevented a buyer from ever realizing a decent rate of return. Hundreds of Western executives hit the ground running, looking for deals, but the vast majority came up empty-handed.

Unilever PLC, the giant food company, amassed an $8 billion war chest in 1997 to make acquisitions in emerging markets. In 1999, it returned the money to shareholders, citing a lack of "acquisition targets that would create value at their current prices." Ford, Lucent Technologies, Chase Manhattan, and others spent considerable time looking for Asian acquisitions, only to return empty-handed. Ted Teng, president of Starwood Hotels' Asian group, summed up the problem, "There is a huge value gap between what buyers (foreigners) are willing to pay and sellers (Asian owners) are willing to take."

My experience drumming up new investments for the $1.8 billion AIG-Asian Infrastructure Fund was similar. In Thailand, the few large firms that weren't technically bankrupt presented regulatory problems, since foreigners were prohibited from owning more than a 25 percent interest in any company operating in 30 key industrial sectors. In South Korea, corporate managers clung to the belief that the drop in asset values was temporary—delaying meaningful negotiations—even as their companies fell into insolvency. In China, the government allowed foreign power project sponsors to lose all of their investments when things went wrong, but the upside, when things went right, was capped at 12 percent to 14 percent. Finding worthwhile investments wasn't easy, as the locals were wary of being exploited by outsiders.

Inexperienced Western firms jump at the chance to buy into a promising emerging market and accept one-sided terms from the local establishment. Such transactions represent an expensive education. China, Russia, and Indonesia—to name three countries—are the graveyards for billions of dollars of Western investment. Just recently, Coca Cola, the big soft drink company, took a $400 million write-down of its Russian assets. Starry-eyed executives who think they are going to make easy money should avoid the developing world.

SEVERE MACROECONOMIC FLUCTUATIONS

To say the value of an emerging market investment is subject to macroeconomic fluctuations is an understatement. Following the hype that saw Western money flood into these countries, there occurred massive currency devaluations and financial crises that rotated through Latin America, Asia, and the former Soviet Union. In U.S. dollar terms, the stock markets of numerous countries dropped by 70 percent or more, a decline not seen in the United States since the Great Depression. Real estate and operating asset values experienced similar declines in these countries. In each case, the transformation from a promising market to an economic basket case was amazingly swift. Facing imminent bankruptcy and a shortage of time, the affected governments didn't settle for the gradualist solutions favored by central bankers. Instead, they received massive bailouts, courtesy of the IMF, World Bank, and G-7 community, whose leaders worried that the daisy chain of catastrophes might attach itself to the financial centers of New York, London, and Tokyo.

Blue-chip banks, investment houses, and operating companies were caught in the maelstrom, sacrificing tens of billions of dollars in the process. Losses were concentrated among the private sector, since sovereign obligations were backed by the multilaterals and G-7 nations. Few of the so-called emerging market "experts" employed by Western banks envisioned the train wreck. Indeed, most had been tireless promoters of the various developing countries up to the day before their respective crashes. Several of the markets eventually bounced back and a portion of the losses were reclaimed. But the damage had been done, and the crises sharply illustrated the risk vis-à-vis safer developed countries, such as the United States and Germany.

These financial upsets were just one part of a long line of dislocations. Such "boom-and-bust" cycles were well-established (see Figure 1.2), and the question remained whether continued integration with Western investors made these poor countries more susceptible to breakdowns, or less. The bailout packages provided damage control and prevented national defaults, thus shielding Western

FIGURE 1.2 Emerging market economies are characterized by "boom and bust" cycles.

investors from greater loses. But this protection encourages more risk taking in the future. The IMF received pressure from the U.S. Congress to discontinue the free insurance policy. As a meager example of its new resolve, the IMF denied a bailout in late 1999 to Ecuador, a small South American nation, forcing it to default on its debts. By late 2000, however, it was business as usual, as the IMF structured multi-billion bailouts for Argentina and Turkey.

From this discussion, it is clear that an emerging market investment contains more pitfalls than a similar commitment to a "developed country." This doesn't mean you should avoid these markets, but it recommends a degree of study, preparation, and caution that is greater than one exercises in a Western setting. Later on in Chapters 4, 7, and 10, we'll discuss methods to manage that risk, as well as the appropriate rates of return for such investments in Chapters 6 through 9.

MULTIPLE OPPORTUNITIES

Despite the dangers that Western companies, banks, and portfolio investors face in the developing nations, there remains a fascination with these exotic locales. The growth potential of the largest of these economies seems endless. In India, a nation of one billion people, only 2 percent of the population has a phone, and only 1 percent own a car. Most Indians are too poor to afford these products, but imagine the increase in demand with a sustained improvement in the economy. Computers sold to an additional 1 percent of the population would provide sales volumes of $20 billion!

On the supply side of the equation, emerging markets are attractive export platforms for multinationals. The wage-and-benefit packages paid to workers are far less than the compensation for similar work in the developed nations, and health, safety, and environmental regulations are either poorly enforced or non-existent. For example, rather than pay an American worker $6.00 per hour to make processed food, Sysco outsources this task to Sigma Alimentos, a Mexican firm that pays its employees $1.00 per hour and then exports the product to the United States. Sure, Mexican productivity is lower and shipping expense is higher with the Mexican tie-in, but the wage differential ensures a benefit to the U.S. company.

My visit to a major textile plant, near Medellin, Columbia, was a stark introduction to the primitive working conditions found in many developing nations. Antiquated equipment in the weaving and dyeing process spread noxious fumes around the plant, and few workers wore protection. Polluted air spread throughout the neighborhood, unfiltered by the plant, and workers casually dropped industrial waste on open grounds outside the site. Chemical-rich effluent then went untreated into the local water table. Trips to factories in Eastern Asia presented decrepit surroundings that were reminiscent of an Industrial Age sweatshop. Local employers are becoming enlightened, but correcting these problems costs money they either don't have or don't care to spend.

In natural resource industries, like oil and gas, timber and mining, emerging markets represent new areas of exploration. With remote locales and rudimentary infrastructures, the developing country's resources are expensive to extract, but the alternative for the multinational is to explore Western sites that have either been picked-over or are subject to stringent environmental laws. That's why less and less oil exploration is being done in the United States. Already, Mexico, Venezuela, and Nigeria, three emerging markets, supply 19 percent of U.S. oil needs, and the Central Asian states near the Caspian Sea will be major suppliers by 2010.

Like big corporations, portfolio investors have several ways to play the emerging markets. Sophisticated institutions can open local brokerage accounts and buy securities directly from the local exchange. Proxy securities called Global Depository Receipts (GDRs) or American Depository Receipts (ADRs), trade on the NYSE and NASDAQ. Telefonos de Mexico and China Unicom are two of the most active issues on the exchanges. Alternatively, investors can buy the securities of multinationals active in the developing world. Coca-Cola, for example, derives 50 percent of its unit volume from developing economies. For those who want to spread their bets on many firms, a variety of mutual funds are available, including country funds, regional funds, and industry-specific funds.

THE EMERGING MARKET QUANDARY

Faced with a wealth of seeming opportunities, corporations, institutions, and individuals are presented with a quandary. Venture into the emerging markets—with each investment possibility accompanied by a special set of risks—or ignore 84 percent of the world's population. It is not an easy choice.

In the 1990s, corporations and individuals made huge sums in the United States, as the domestic economy took off. A large number of these participants never gave a thought to going overseas, where customs and languages are strange; and, frankly speaking, it's harder to do business. More importantly, people don't like to lose money, and the emerging markets show no guarantee of a good investment return. From 1990 to 2000, for example, the IFC investable index provided a compound annual rate of return (in US$) of 6 percent. The comparable return of the popular S&P 500 index was 19 percent, with less price volatility, no political risk and little currency fluctuation.

On the other hand, risk taking is part of a forward-looking business profile, and staying close to home is not always a good long-term move. A sensible strategy is striking a balance between the rich, developed markets and the poor, developing countries. As you examine their relative economic firepower, you'll see that even the largest emerging markets are destined to be niche plays. For example, the economy of Poland, with 39 million people, is equal to the economy of the state of Maryland, with a population of 5 million, while India (population, 1 billion) has less gross domestic product than California.

Narrowing Your Focus

U.S. companies and investment funds focus their efforts on the 12 largest emerging markets, which collectively represent 73 percent of the segment's GDP:

Argentina	Poland
Brazil	Russia
China	South Africa
India	South Korea
Indonesia	Thailand
Mexico	Turkey

These 12 larger economies are sensible places of entry for the newcomer. Other Western firms have paved the way and a certain infrastructure is established for foreigners to do business. By consulting Western banks, law firms, and companies with operations there, a multinational can assemble a team to plan an entry and implement it. Including local lawyers and consultants, the team is familiar with the bureaucratic red tape, regulatory obstacles, requisite political and business connections, and legal formalities. In this way, the foreigner doesn't "reinvent the wheel" and thus avoids wasting time and money. Remember, playing by these rules doesn't guarantee a successful market entry or thriving supply platform—even when your product line is superior or your cost structure is lower than the local competition. Frequently, a good business plan needs something "extra."

Beware of Differences

Dispatched by an American consulting firm to open a Buenos Aires office, a Latin friend of mine was frustrated in securing consulting contracts from local utilities, despite his company's superiority over the domestic players. After nine months of coming up empty—with nothing to offer headquarters by way of explanation—he consulted a business official at the U.S. Embassy. "Oh, you want to win contracts!" said the official, "you'll need to see so and so; he's an American and he's been here 20 years." My friend met with the intermediary, and afterwards, his firm started winning contracts. At 10 percent to 15 percent of the contract value, the intermediary's price was steep. A large portion of his fee was paid out in questionable commissions, but my friend was finally able to show revenue for the executives back home.

For the portfolio investor, the larger stock markets have a semblance of order, although they've a long way to go before approaching the New York Stock Exchange. The big stocks trading on these exchanges have an acceptable amount of activity, so investors can move in and out them without upsetting the price, but abuses that have been largely wrung out of the American system—insider trading, phony accounting, and front running—are still prevalent. As you proceed to the smaller stock markets, liquidity, fairness, and transparency diminish further, and speculative elements dominate securities trading.

SUMMARY

Emerging markets represent the bulk of the world's population but only a fraction of its economic output. Many of the markets are attractive export platforms, and a smaller group of large states offer opportunities for in-country sales growth. Moneymaking opportunities in the emerging markets involve special risks that are not prominent in United States or Western European deals.

CHAPTER 2

What Is an Emerging Market?

Emerging markets are poor countries with per capita incomes of less than $9,000. 156 nations fit this definition, encompassing 84 percent of the world's population and 75 percent of sovereign states. Most have per capita incomes of less than $3,000, which translates into an average household income of $4,000. This small amount supports four people on about $3 per person per day. Other labels for these countries include developing nations, low-income countries, and the Third World. By way of comparison, the United States has a per capita income of $30,000, and a median household income of $38,000. (This translates to $28.50 per person per day for a four-person family.)

On the basis of their economic importance alone, the emerging markets are not a major force, representing only 20 percent of global GNP. Their small share of the world's income is spread over 156 countries, versus a much large proportion divided among 54 developed nations. The largest three emerging economies—China, Brazil, and Russia—provide only 7 percent of global GNP. In contrast, the top three developed countries—the United States, Japan, and Germany—contribute 49 percent.

The wealthier countries are described as developed countries, Western economies, and the First World. They have per capital incomes in excess of $9,000 and maintain substantial industrial bases. For the most part, this term refers to the United States, Canada, and Western Europe, together with Japan, Australia, and New Zealand.

The words "developing country" and "developed country" don't do justice to the dramatic differences between the two classes of economy. For people who haven't traveled extensively, it is difficult to visualize the grinding poverty afflicting most developing countries. Things most of us take for granted in the United States—a telephone, a decent home, and a family car—are not within the means of the average breadwinner in developing nations. Well-paying jobs are scarce and economic advancement opportunities are limited, as wealth is concentrated in the hands of a small elite who promote a rigid class structure. The sharp differences are described by Eduardo Doryan, Vice President of Human Development for the World Bank. The problem in places such as India, "is that you'll see at least two countries, one where most people are on a boat heading back to the nineteenth century and another where the boat is heading to the twenty-first century." See Figure 2.1.

These poor nations have no proprietary technology and little in the way of an industrial base. Many business sectors have been untouched by technology for dozens of years, and capital equipment is frequently inefficient and antiquated. One chemical plant I visited in Venezuela had process controls from the 1960s. The poor nations' economies are dominated by agriculture, and the landscapes outside of the few large cities are dotted with small farms, where families eke out a subsistence living as people did hundreds of years ago.

Despite the efforts of multiple aid organizations, involving dozens of years and hundreds of billions of dollars, only a handful of these countries have "graduated" from "developing" to "developed" status. Recent setbacks caused by the currency crises of the 1990s reversed much of the progress made years earlier.

ARE EMERGING MARKETS IMPORTANT?

In contrast to their small economic contribution, the emerging markets attract considerable attention from Western governments and businesses. From a geopolitical view, certain emerging markets sit

FIGURE 2.1 Emerging markets have stark divides between the few rich, and the many poor.

astride important shipping lanes and sensitive border areas. Several have large armies and substantial arsenals, which, when combined with a lack of political stability and recurrent xenophobia, present the wealthier countries with spill-over problems that they would like to avoid. For this reason, the West put tremendous resources into resolving the Bosnian conflict, which was near Western Europe, and into reversing Iraq's takeover of Kuwait, which was a major Western oil supplier.

Important Suppliers of Raw Materials

From a business point of view, emerging markets supply the materials necessary to keep the industrialized economies running. For example, Nigeria, Mexico, Venezuela, Indonesia, and several Middle Eastern countries are major sources of oil—still the most vital energy source for the First World. Similarly, Papua New Guinea, Jamaica, Brazil, Russia, and China supply half of the world's bauxite (aluminum ore), and emerging markets provide over half of the production of other key minerals such as copper, tin, iron, manganese, and chromium. If the flow of these supplies were to be cut off for only a few months, the developed economies would experience a severe dislocation, if not an unbridled panic.

Looking to the future, the supplier role of the developing countries will expand since the exploitation of natural resources in many of the wealthy countries has reached its limit. Either the oil fields, mines, or forests have been tapped out, or environmental regulations reduce new exploration and development. In the United States, for example, the proportion of oil needs supplied by domestic wells has steadily declined, and the trend is similar for other raw materials, such as tin, cobalt, nickel, and chromium.

Providers of Inexpensive Labor

In addition to the natural resource element, the Third World is a good source of low-cost, unskilled labor. Large corporations transfer their assembly and production plants from developed locations to these areas, and save significantly on labor costs. Furthermore, as wage and education levels rise in the West, multinationals have difficulty attracting workers to low-paying, repetitive production jobs, thus promoting the continuation of plant transfers. From the United States, the textile industry has moved to the low-wage Asian countries, demonstrating how the First World relies on cheap labor. Should the emerging markets suddenly stop providing workers to the multinationals, the expense of making goods locally would significantly increase the cost of living in the United States and Europe.

Markets for Western Products

The emerging markets purchase substantial amounts of Western goods and services. Local businesses use imported machinery, and complex software and production processes are derived from Western patents. However, the small size of these economies—on an individual basis—make them secondary markets for the big multinationals. At the consumer level, low per-capita incomes suggest that the demand for anything but basic staples and inexpensive notions is limited. Commenting on China's ability to buy expensive products, Alan Tonelson, a research fellow at the U.S. Business and Industry Council, notes, "The notion that there's a big consumer market (in China) for goods made in the United States is, I think, pie-in-the-sky."

The World Bank describes the better-off members of the developing world as "upper middle-income," with annual per capita GNP of $3,000 to $9,000. The middle-income category has GOP of $725 to $3,000 per capita, and the low income countries fall under $725. The number of countries and population in each grouping are shown in Table 2.1.

Most residents of "low-income" nations operate on a subsistence level and lack access to modern requirements, such as potable water, electricity, schooling, and health care. Ed Roston, a former executive at Seven-Up, recalls, "When we (Phillip Morris) first did a market study in Brazil, we found out that two-thirds of the people couldn't

TABLE 2.1 Segmenting Emerging Markets by Income Category

	Number of Countries	Population (Millions)
Upper middle income	61	2,036
Middle income	59	2,283
Low income	36	574
Total	156	4,893

afford soda!" As the income levels rise, citizens achieve necessities, and the demand for nonessential goods climbs, particularly in the larger cities, where the society is more advanced than in the countryside. In Beijing, for example, locals can be found wearing American-style T-shirts and Nike athletic shoes. In the outlying Hubei province, you rarely see these products. Even so, estimates show that only about 10 percent of China's 1.3 billion people can afford Western products like Crest toothpaste and Gatorade.

The dynamics of the poor nations supplying the Western countries, as opposed to buying Western goods, are illustrated in Table 2.2, which shows the trade surpluses enjoyed by developing nations against the United States. China, for example, sold $82 billion worth of goods to the United States in 1999, yet imported only $13 billion.

Over the long-term, the United States and other developed nations expect the trade deficits to moderate, as the Third World grows out of its supplier role and becomes a larger consumer of Western goods. Although the potential is there, the progress is likely to come in fits and starts. Even at a continuous high rate of growth, say 6 percent, it would take a relatively prosperous country, like Argentina, 50 years to reach the level of the United States. Don't expect this growth to come easily. In the past, these nations clung to statist or socialistic economic policies that tended to retard economic growth rather than foster it. The failure of these policies

TABLE 2.2 1999 Balance of Trade Surplus with U.S., Top 10 Emerging Market Trading Partners (in Billions)

Mexico	$23*
China	69
South Korea	8
Malaysia	12
Brazil	(2)
Venezuela	6
Thailand	9
Philippines	5
Indonesia	7
India	4

*Excludes drug trade estimated at several billion.
Source: U.S. Census Bureau Merchandise Trade Report.

and, later, the fall of communism, brought about economic liberalization, but the road to stable capitalism has not been smooth. Asian countries such as Indonesia and Malaysia, "emerged" from stagnation to post strong growth, only to experience sharp reversals. In Europe, Russia ended communism and attracted billions of dollars to its privatizing economy, only to default on its debts in 1998. In contrast, Poland and Estonia made steady progress in the 1990s in spite of others' setbacks.

CONTINUING IMPORTANCE OF EMERGING MARKETS

Given the current state of affairs, the emerging economies deserve the attention of Western corporations. Besides their geopolitical importance, they are significant actors in the global economy, although destined for secondary roles.

Emerging markets' attributes that interest western multinationals include:

- ▪ Strategic importance.
- ▪ Raw material supply.
- ▪ Inexpensive labor force.
- ▪ Existing markets for Western goods.
- ▪ Potential for economic growth and broader demand for Western products.

As these countries progress, they'll need continued access to Western capital, technology, and managerial skill. The ease of this access will depend, in large part, on the willingness of local elites to surrender portions of their hard-won independence, since multinationals refuse to commit large sums without exercising a good deal of control over their investments. The interaction of the developed countries with the multinationals comes at a price, as it always has.

BRIEF HISTORY

The history of the developed nations mixing with First World businesses dates back centuries. Long-distance trade can be traced to Marco Polo, but sustained entries started around 1500 when Europeans established navigable sea routes around South Africa and across the Atlantic to North and South America. Holland and England made significant inroads into Asia in the sixteenth century, and England and France were colonizing several fronts in North America. By the mid 1700s, large portions of what we now call the "emerging markets' were colonies of the European powers. By the mid 1800s, independence movements decolonized most of the Americas, and the European powers focused their efforts on previously unexplored areas of Africa. By 1900, Africa was effectively controlled by European nations.

The 1900s saw the colonial system disintegrate. The cost of defending their rules became too costly for the European states, and revolutions and nationalistic movements put pressure on the powers to disband their empires. Today, the traditional colony has effectively disappeared, although poor countries complain that neocolonialism has taken its place. They view themselves as politically independent, but their ability to control their own development and destiny is compromised and constrained by the actions of Western states, transnational corporations and international financial agencies.

The criticism is renewed when a multilateral lender such as the International Monetary Fund (IMF) imposes restrictive economic policies on a developing country in exchange for a loan. The situation is akin to a doctor prescribing bad-tasting medicine for a cold. It may be good for you, but you don't like to take it. In South Korea, for example, the local media and governmental officialdom falsely blamed the nation's troubles on the IMF (which had kept the country out of bankruptcy), and the Korean citizenry used it as a rhetorical punching bag. In downtown Seoul, for example, in 1998, I observed numerous advertisements for a bare lunch of "bread and water," featured as the "IMF Special."

At other times, the developing nations fight the rich economies. The Organization of Petroleum Exporting Countries (OPEC) was formed in 1960 by 11 oil exporting nations to coordinate their negotiations with the Western oil companies. This cartel has met with comparative success and continues to manipulate the supply and price of oil, but OPEC is a glaring exception. The developing nations are generally too fragmented to act as a collective on economic matters. Besides disorganization and ego problems, their small individual economies, relative to the developed countries, limit the practicality of unilateral action. As a result, the wealthy nations maintain an inherent trading advantage, using their superior market positions to gain economic power.

HISTORY AS AN EXCUSE FOR LACK OF PROGRESS

As an American traveling to emerging markets, I wondered why most developing countries stalled on the road to economic progress. Many are richly endowed with natural resources, acceptable climates, and manageable population densities—not unlike the United States in the late 1800s. The colonial yoke, in most instances, was thrown off decades previously, so the countries had been free to operate in their own best interests.

Latin American countries, for example, were independent within several decades of the American Revolution of 1776. Yet, over 150 years later, their economies are nowhere near the United States. In conversations about this phenomenon, World Bank authorities reel off reasons for the stagnation—such as poor macroeconomic environments, lack of capital investments, and no rule of law—but no one knows exactly why the governing classes allow these dismal situations to fester.

The emerging market executive looks outward to explain the problem, rather than examining his country's shortcomings. The most popular patsy is a colonial legacy. A common excuse sounds like this: "You (Westerners) never taught us to build an economy or follow the rules! You just taught us how to make a quick buck!" This explanation would be laughable if I hadn't heard it so many times. Not only does it ignore the long time separating colonialism from the present day, but it glosses over the fact that most of the people running those economies visit the West regularly. Some hold degrees from Western universities.

The resistance to progress is exemplified by Mexico. Despite bordering the world's largest economy for dozens of years, exporting its own people there, and absorbing much of the U.S. culture, very little of the United States' economic dynamism rubs-off on Mexico. The country is poor, with a per capita GNP just one-eighth of the United States. As in many developing countries, the government is corrupt, and the country is bloated with foreign debts.

RECOGNIZE THE DIFFERENCES

Even as we have lumped 156 countries into one group called "emerging markets," note these nations are extremely diverse, not only among economic and business lines, which are the focus of this book, but also among historical, cultural, political, and religious attributes.

Economic Prosperity

For example, the principal income marker—below $9,000 per capita—covers a wide range of circumstances. At the high end is South Korea, with a per capita income of $8,900. It has office and apartment buildings with the feel of the American Midwest, and the roads are well-paved and filled with modern cars. Koreans are well-fed, well-dressed, and well-equipped with cell phones and Sony Walkmans. At the bottom of the range lies Somalia, with a per capita income of $120. The main cities are ramshackle affairs, with crumbling office buildings and pot-holed streets. Electricity reaches a small minority of homes for only several hours a day. The few cars on the road are beaten-up jalopies that share passage with pedestrians, bicycles, farm animals, and horse-drawn wagons. Health care, schooling, and related government services are meager to non-existent, and the majority of the populace is tied to the land, living a lifestyle that is a throwback to feudal times.

Languages

The 156 emerging markets support dozens of primary languages and hundreds of dialects. Countries that Westerners might consider small, like Vietnam, have their own languages, the vocabulary and grammar of which is distinct from Chinese or Malay. This puts Western businessmen at a disadvantage, since they're reluctant to study the language of small markets, like Vietnam, when there's more business to be done in a larger country with one principal idiom, such as Russia. Countries in Sub-Saharan Africa, like Nigeria, a nation of 120 million people, have dozens of languages in everyday use, spoken by the large number of tribes that comprise this nation.

English is the international language, and most senior level executives with whom I've worked in developing nations speak passable English. A good many of them received training in Western schools or executive programs.

Unique Cultures

Where the language is uniform throughout the region, the Westerner must remember that each country has a separate identity. Telefonica, the Spanish phone company, makes more money in Latin America than it does in Spain, and Mateo Budinich, General Manager, relates the success of Telefonica there as follows, "We have a shared language, but each nation is extremely different in Latin America. The Spanish are sensitive to that, while at the same time capitalizing on the similarities in our cultures to smooth the way in business deals."

Thus, as we discuss the commonalities of emerging markets, it is helpful to remember that each is a unique business environment. Western investors must study the landscape before making a commitment.

POLITICAL FRAMEWORK

Only a handful of the emerging markets approach the freedom and openness of the U.S. and Western European democracies. On the other hand, most are not oppressive military dictatorships, so the vast majority fit somewhere in between. Many are making transitions to multiparty democratic rule. In 2000, for example, Taiwan, Mexico, and Nigeria ousted long-time ruling parties.

Even in the quasi-democracies, freedom of the press is restricted, and you can hardly pick up a *Washington Post, Wall Street Journal,* or *Financial Times* without seeing an emerging market government harass a media outlet that has become too critical of the ruling class. In the first two months of 2000, for example, Hungary shut down a television station, Malaysia closed a newspaper, and Russia arrested correspondents. Over the course of a year, the list of such actions covers several printed pages.

For countries with authoritarian regimes, the system exercises significant control over economic activities, as well as having a hand in everyday life. In China, for example, the average person cannot change residences without an official permission, and educated citizens are assigned jobs by the State, rather than seeking positions of their own choice. Permits and licenses for new businesses go through a web of local, municipal, provincial, and national bureaucracies, which often act at cross-purposes. And since the media is closely monitored by government, a foreigner takes what he sees in local newspapers and television shows with a grain of salt, as stories that reflect badly on the administration never see the light of day.

By and large, it's best for a foreign businessman to steer clear of political discussions when traveling to an emerging market. In the authoritarian countries, local executives are afraid to discuss current affairs, because frankness or criticism regarding the existing regime might get back to those in power and invite reprisal. Even minor people are subject to harassment. In China, one of my guides was subjected to policemen barging into her hotel room at 3 A.M., and questioning her for several hours. In the multiparty systems that govern most of the larger emerging markets (for example, Brazil, India, Turkey, and Russia), behind-the-scenes dealings have special importance, and executives keep their political leanings close to the vest. Elected officials can dispense more favors than their U.S. counterparts, so a businessman doesn't want to be in front of a cause should his side lose. Discussing political matters with an outsider is not a practical option.

CORRUPTION

When an international businessman meets a government official in an emerging market, his first instinct is to "Westernize" the individual. If the official is a bureaucrat in a government ministry, you believe, at first glance, that he is an underpaid civil servant, dutifully following laws and procedures with an eye toward providing quality municipal service. If the official is an elected politician, you consider him as an underpaid ideologue, fighting for the little man. In both cases, you're likely to be more wrong than right. The sad truth is that the tradition of public service is not well established in these places. Too many politicians and civil servants in the developing countries view a government career as akin to a private sector job, with one primary goal in mind—making money. Victor Alderete, for example, the director of Argentina's Pensioners Health Care Agency, misappropriated a fortune from the agency, buying luxuries like a $1 million ranch in Uruguay. Moria Julia Alsogaray, head of the environmental agency, was caught skimming millions from her budget. Since public sector jobs have low salaries and no stock options—as compared to a private position—the difference is made up, unfortunately, by bribes and insider deals. Public employees and elected officials accept these prerequisites in exchange for government contracts, licenses, and privileges.

Many individuals who reach the upper pinnacles of developing country administrations amass huge fortunes—with no questions asked. Carlos "Hank" Rhon worked in several Mexican administrations, never earning more than $200,000 per year over several decades, yet Forbes magazine places his personal net worth at $1 billion. Mr. Rhon coined the phrase, "a politician who is poor is a poor politician." Sani Abacha Mobutu, the former dictator of Nigeria, had $3 billion in Swiss bank accounts at the time of his death in 1998, and the government of Indonesia is still trying to retrieve the $5 billion accumulated by the Suharto family during its time in power.

With many of the top officials setting a poor example, low-level bureaucrats are active in demanding payments for business licenses, permits, and concessions. Corruption in zoning laws is legendary. With few exceptions, emerging markets cities are a morass of incongruous architecture—congregated tin shacks next to office buildings adjacent to a strip mall next to a run-down health service. The malaise drifts down to the clerical personnel. In Kenya, for example, an assistant in the Department of Motor Vehicles refuses you a driver's license application unless she receives a "tip."

Not surprisingly, the attitude of local residents toward govern-ment and politics is cynical. They respond by hiding income to avoid paying taxes. Phony invoices and offshore accounts shield payments due the government for import duties and corporate taxes. Less so-phisticated residents emphasize cash or barter transactions. The un-derground economy can amount to as much as 50 percent of GDP in an emerging market.

SYSTEM OF LAW ENFORCEMENT

One of the first things a Western traveler notices in an emerging mar-ket is the proliferation of metal bars, which seem to cover every win-dow, door, and gate. At the same time, buildings, parking lots, banks, large stores, and wealthy homes routinely have private guards circling the grounds, giving the impression that these places are under siege. The root problem is a law enforcement system that is ineffective against minor property crimes like burglary, so people protect their possessions themselves. Violent crime, on a per capita basis, is lower than the United States because access to guns is more tightly re-stricted. That being said, crime statistics are biased toward the low side, as most victims don't bother to report illegalities to the police (see Figure 2.2).

CURRENCY

A nation's currency is a proxy for its financial and political stability. For example, the strongest currency in the world, the Swiss Franc, is admin-istered by Switzerland, a model of consistency in government and fi-nance. Switzerland has had the same representative democracy for 153 years, and its government finances are beyond reproach. These dual qualities have made the country—and its currency—a haven for millions of investors over the years, and Switzerland has become a mega banking center, despite the country's small population of 7 million.

FIGURE 2.2   Emerging market residents are very concerned about personal security.

The U.S. dollar ranks high everywhere as a solid currency. Although it has depreciated over the years relative to the Swiss Franc, the dollar is a mainstay of international commerce, due largely to the size of the U.S. economy. Broad-based commodities such as oil and paper are priced in U.S. dollars, and many international transactions, irrespective of location, are priced or indexed to the dollar. This custom includes the business sector, as well as the man-on-the-street. In every emerging market that I visit, the U.S. dollar is a de facto substitute currency. People accept U.S. dollars for routine purchases such as taxi rides and meals. This practice is technically illegal, but it continues, as residents show a marked preference for the greenback.

CURRENCY DEVALUATION

The desire for U.S. money rather than the local currency is the product of common sense. History illustrates that emerging market currencies do not hold their value. People living in these countries know this fact and they act accordingly. Low-income residents hoard U.S. dollars and accumulate hard assets that hold value, such as gold jewelry. In Russia, for example, the government acknowledges a large part of domestic

FIGURE 2.3   Emerging market residents often prefer to hoard U.S. dollars, rather than place their savings in the local currency.

savings is not invested locally; rather, it's tucked away in large U.S. bills in mattresses (see Figure 2.3). Wealthy people maintain offshore accounts, and this situation is reflected by the large number of emerging market firms that issue Eurobonds. In the 1990s, for example, most Korean convertible bonds were sold in Switzerland. The buyers were the flight capital accounts of rich Koreans.

The performance of major emerging market currencies against the U.S. dollar is what convinces people to go offshore. Table 2.3 illustrates how many currencies have devaluated by 80 percent or more.

Rather than attack the principal causes of currency depreciation, the developing country government goes for cosmetics. After a few years of declining currency value, it might print a new currency that lops off two zeros from the denomination of the older currency. In 1993, for example, Mexico invented the new peso, which was worth 1000 old pesos. These superficial actions diminish investor confidence, but they have a practical component. Cash registers and blank checks only have room for so many zeros, and it's easier to process transactions at 10 pesos than 10,000.

TABLE 2.3   Currency Value Depreciation (in Percent) against U.S. Dollar

	Last 10 Years 1989–1999	Last 20 Years 1979–1999
Asia		
Chinese yuan	43	82
India rupee	62	83
South Korea won	39	57
Latin America		
Colombian peso	80	98
Mexican peso	72	81
Venezuelan bolivar	94	99
Europe		
Hungarian forint	78	87
Polish zloty	85	99
African		
Egyptian pound	68	80
South African rand	65	88

For foreigners dealing in cash, a new currency saves storage space in the wallet. During a trip to Guyana, a small impoverished nation on the South American coast, my exchange of a single US$100 bill into the local currency produced a one-inch stack of Guyanese bills totaling G$5,000. The local currency was depreciating so fast that the government couldn't print large denominations fast enough, so I was stuck with dozens of G$20 and G$50 bills.

CAUSES OF DEVALUATIONS

The weakness of emerging market currency regimes stems from a lack of fiscal and monetary discipline. The central governments like to spend more money than they take in from taxes, fees, and custom duties. Since their poor credit ratings prevent them from borrowing substantial sums, they obtain the funds by essentially printing money to cover the difference. They have the central bank expand the currency base by acquiring more government bonds (i.e., lending the government more money). In Western nations, independent central banks restrain this political merry-go-round, but the central banks of developing nations are under the direct control of the elected politicians who are doing the spending. The end result is currency expansion, high inflation rates (30 percent to 40 percent annually is not unusual) and repeated devaluations.

With the demand for its currency being less than robust, the average Third World country supports its currency by imposing restrictions on its free exchange into U.S. dollars, Japanese yen, or similar hard currencies. On the high end, a large foreign corporation that needs to exchange local currency for millions of U.S. dollars fills out a government form, and then waits in a queue. The length of the wait depends on U.S. dollar availability. Sometimes, multiple exchange rates are offered by the government, based on the use of the money and the timing of the exchange. On the low end, a vacationing tourist pays the official rate for local money (and completes bogus paperwork), when black market transactions a block from his hotel involve a substantial discount. On my first trip to Egypt, I saved hundreds of dollars by using street-side moneychangers.

Several emerging markets have truly open foreign exchange markets, such as Argentina and Mexico, but these countries are the exception rather than the rule. Even then, trading activity in dated securities, such as government bonds, invokes skepticism as to whether such a regime can hold. For example, Argentina's peso is 100 percent linked to the U.S. dollar, but six-month Argentine T-bills trade 3 percent higher than the U.S. counterpart. Why? History shows that few countries have the discipline to maintain such systems, and investors are wary of Argentina's ability to stay the course. That's why only a handful of developing countries have active futures markets.

BOND MARKETS

With neither locals nor foreigners having faith in a currency's forward worth, a developing nation's capital markets are short-term oriented. Investors don't want to lose money over the unpredictable long-term, so trading is dominated by 3- to 6-month treasury bills, certificates of deposit, and commercial paper. The rare long-term debt instrument has a floating rate designed to insulate the holder against changing interest levels. For example, the longest fixed-rate bond available in Brazil, a major emerging market, is nine months.

Without a functioning bond market, a developing nation is vulnerable to shocks. Businesses are overly reliant on short-term loans from commercial banks, which themselves depend on the continued rollover of short-term deposits. The banks then take a seemingly conservative posture and concentrate their loans to either (1) large, established firms, which have an audited track record, or (2) property developers, which provide so-called "hard" collateral in the form of land, bricks, and mortar. For these chosen customers, this easy money from the banks invariably leads to over-borrowing and lousy investment decisions. As the poor investment returns and property losses among the leveraged borrowers become evident, confidence in the banks' portfolios weakens, and depositors—particularly the large foreign depositors—gradually withdraw their funding. A financial panic ensues and the currency devaluation cycle begins.

The lack of a bond market has specific repercussions for the average breadwinner. Since lenders are reluctant to commit on a long-term basis, there are no 15-, 20-, or 30-year mortgages available for wage earners. The prospective homeowner must come up with substantial cash, like 50 percent to 75 percent of a home's purchase price, or he is consigned to renting a residence. Home ownership promotes stability in society and a belief that the owner has a stake in his country's future. Without it, developing nations face problems in getting citizens to buy into the system.

THE STOCK MARKET

Equity trading is volatile and speculative in nature. Investors can't rely on the Warren Buffet style of studying a stock and holding it for the long haul; it is too easy for macroeconomic forces to overwhelm the individual company analysis. Furthermore, emerging market accounting is suspect and stock exchanges are lax in enforcing disclosure rules. Even with careful study, an investor relies heavily on educated guesswork. More often than not, people are betting blind, giving the stock markets a casino mentality (see Figure 2.4). In the space of one year, wild trading swings can take place. In 1999, for example, Venezuela's stock market climbed 30 percent, fell 26 percent, and then rose 32 percent.

With the stock market viewed as a game of chance, local investors are reluctant to commit large sums to equities. Mutual funds play a small to nonexistent role in individual's saving schemes, and institutional investors, like insurance companies, avoid stocks. The implications for economic development are problematic. Without access to risk capital, entrepreneurs are stymied and innovation is attenuated. Sophisticated Third World innovators remedy this situation by going public abroad. Roberto Cibrian-Campay, CEO of Brazilian

FIGURE 2.4 Emerging markets are typified by stock market speculation, as opposed to careful analysis.

high-tech firm, El Sitio, explains his desire to seek foreign capital, "In Latin America, business people and investors . . . do not understand the concept of a start-up." Starmedia and Yupi, Latin America's pioneering Internet portals, both completed their IPOs in the United States. Unfortunately, this sort of cross-border financing is the exception rather than the rule.

VENTURE CAPITAL

Venture capital markets in developing countries are small to nonexistent, reflecting the dominance of commercial banks and the concentration of equity capital in the hands of a select group of wealthy families. Successful start-ups are frequently offshoots of these family-run operations, rather than companies begun in garages by true innovators. For example, Zip.net, S.A., the Brazilian Internet firm that was sold for $365 million to Portugal Telecom, was founded by Marcos Moraes, the son of one of Brazil's richest men, Olacyr de Moras. Richard Li, the founder of the Chinese Internet firm, Pacific Century, got his start in business with $125 million in seed money from his father, the patriarch of the Li family holdings, which represent over one-quarter of the Hong Kong stock market. The shortage of institutional risk capital draws many Third World entrepreneurs to the United States and Western Europe, promoting a "brain drain" from these poor nations at a time when dynamic individuals are needed at home.

The rudimentary nature of the Third World capital market inhibits economic development and promotes wealth concentration. The inefficiency creates opportunities for foreigners, but true wealth creation faces obstacles. Even after a success, liquefying an investment is difficult. It's difficult to "exit" an emerging market venture via an initial public offering, and the prospective sale of a local business confronts a limited pool of buyers dominated by the principal family groups. Local governments are making modest steps toward modernization, but real change proceeds slowly.

SOCIAL ORGANIZATION

The average reader of this book resides in North America or Western Europe. These regions have a high percentage of people who are considered "middle class." They live in comfortable economic surroundings—including a modern home, car, and similar conveniences—and hold jobs paying salaries that exceed the costs of the basic necessities. More often than not, the middle-class jobholder has a nest egg, and he is not living from paycheck to paycheck. In the United States, the definition of middle class covers over 80 percent of the population. In Germany, this percentage exceeds 90 percent. A large middle class is conducive to social stability and participatory democracy.

The level of material possessions for a middle-class family in an emerging market is substantially less than the United States or Germany, because the developing nation's overall wealth is lower. However, the basic thrust is the same; the middle-class is an anchor for stability, even in a poor society. Unfortunately, emerging markets don't have a sizable middle class. The typical developing nation is characterized by a small group of elite families enjoying tremendous wealth, and a vast underclass living hand to mouth. Consider Brazil, Latin America's most populous nation. Three percent of the population owns two-thirds of the land. One Peruvian described Latin America to me as follows: "We're essentially a feudal society. There are two classes: nobility and peasant. There's little upward mobility, so we don't have a middle class. Rights and privileges pass through the traditional wealthy families."

To reduce the poor's resentment, to minimize social unrest, and to avoid kidnappings, ostentatious displays of wealth—outside of residences—are discouraged in Latin America. In safer countries, rich Latin Americans can be more indulgent. For example, many own lavish apartments in New York City and Miami. Oswaldo Cisneros, scion of Venezuela's Cisneros family, recently sold his Upper East Side townhouse for $12 million. The Cisneros Group controls more than 50 companies in Latin America, the United States, and Europe.

Parallels are evident in Asian and African countries. In Zimbabwe, for example, 70,000 white farmers own three-quarters of the land in a country of 13 million people. In Indonesia, ethnic Chinese make up 4 percent of the population, but control the bulk of private wealth.

Besides an ossified class structure, these societies confront other developmental obstacles, including racism, tribalism, sexism, and religious discrimination. Where an emerging market is comprised of several races, discrimination by the dominant race tends to be more pronounced than in the West. In Latin America, for example, Indians (indigenous peoples) and mestizos (indigenous/white mixed) represent 80 percent to 90 percent of the population, yet they have little representation in the executive ranks. In six years in corporate finance, less than one in 50 Latin executives I met were Indians or mestizos. The media perpetuates the discrimination. Virtually every advertisement features white-skinned models, and the popular television soap operas are filled with Caucasian actors.

Tribalism is evident in developing countries, particularly in Africa, where people feel more loyalty to their tribe than to their race or country. This feeling manifests itself in discrimination from tribe to tribe and fragmentation among different tribal groups. The tragedies in Rwanda were an outgrowth of tribalism, as the Hutu/Tutsi rivalry ended in bloodshed that the U.N. forces couldn't stop.

Sexism is prevalent in developing countries, and women are routinely denied schooling, career options, and civil rights. In rural India, for example, women can be murdered by their husbands for adultery, with the guilty man facing no penalty. In parts of rural China, statistics show 10 percent more male than female births. The difference is attributable to female babies being killed at birth or aborted in the womb (ultrasound can indicate sex before birth). In Africa, governments allow girls to be withdrawn from school much earlier than boys. In too many of these nations, male attitudes toward a women's place in society are a throwback to far earlier times in the First World.

Religious intolerance is a problem in the Third World, and it causes many armed conflicts. Recent actions in Bosnia, East Timor, and Philippines stemmed from religious differences.

The forces of class, racism, tribalism, sexism, and religious discrimination are more pronounced in developing nations than in Westernized nations. A key function of local armies is simply to maintain order among the factions. The spread of Western culture, which increasingly promotes equality and tolerance, weakens these backward forces, but the modernization process takes time.

SUMMARY

An emerging market is a poor country with a limited industrial base. A high proportion of economic activity is dedicated to agriculture, and a small group of wealthy families tends to dominate business and politics. The job of establishing the systems and infrastructure for a modern market economy is a work-in-progress. Investors are subject to periodic financial panics that result in currency devaluations and deep recessions.

Each of the 156 emerging markets is a distinct country with its own identity and culture. Similarities abound from the business perspective, but each country has unique features that defy generalization.

CHAPTER 3

Business Climate

From a business point of view, Westerners should consider the emerging markets as a walled castle, surrounded by a moat (see Figure 3.1). The fortifications are designed to keep foreign companies at bay, and to protect the local establishment. Without significant barriers to entry, leading businesses would be overrun by multinational corporations, which by virtue of their size and efficiency, would either buy-out the locals or compete them out of existence. For many reasons, the movers and shakers in these developing nations don't want this to happen.

Consider Thailand, for example. Before the Asian financial crisis broke in 1997, its economy was booming, and its cement industry was experiencing double-digit growth, as demand for new roads and buildings surged. The big multinational cement companies—Blue Circle (U.K.), Cemex (Mexico), Holderbank (Switzerland), and La-Farge (France)—were dying to enter the Thai market, but federal law made cement a "strategic industry," akin to military jet engines or supercomputers in the United States. The strategic connotation prohibited foreigners from owning more than 25 percent of a cement business, and it also applied to numerous other mundane industries such as coal mining and agriculture.

This restriction guaranteed the local oligopoly's profits, and it represented one of the foundations of the Ratanarak family's wealth and prestige. They controlled Siam City Cement, a 12 million ton-per-year producer and one of the largest firms on the Bangkok Stock Exchange. Size is relative, however, as SCC's equity capitalization

FIGURE 3.1   An emerging market is like a castle surrounded by a moat, with foreign firms having a difficult time gaining entry.

was only one-twentieth of Blue Circle's. As the crisis ensued, the company's finances sunk under the weight of $600 million of debt, mostly denominated in U.S. dollars. Banks demanded payment and insisted the family find an investor with deep pockets. With potential Thai partners in similar straits, the family—after months of dragging its feet—broke a long-standing taboo of the Thai business establishment;

it brokered a regulatory change with the government and sold control to a foreigner.

For the company's president, Somkiart Limsong, the results were saddening. Before the deal, foreign banks and suppliers showered him with attention, and local newspapers followed his every move. Replaced by a mere division manager of Holderbank, he has no power base and vastly diminished prestige. To Bangkok's elite, he stands as a living testament to the perils of an open market.

To avoid Somkiart's fate, emerging market business leaders are more than willing to forego the economic development and technological advances brought by foreigners. That's one reason so many of these countries are run down. Halfway measures such as joint ventures and licensing agreements involve less of a control give-up, but multinationals are reluctant to hand over money and technology when they're not in a control position.

Supporting these at-home instincts are the legacies of import substitution schemes and socialistic economic policies. In the 1960s and 1970s, the World Bank and other multilaterals encouraged poor nations to develop "homegrown" industries that replaced Western imports. These firms became important symbols of sovereignty, and local officials were reluctant to cut the subsidies and to place the firms and their employees at risk. While the privatization craze has reduced the number of parastatals, the concept of self-sufficiency and local control has been hard to break, and it plays into the hands of the oligopolists.

From the 1960s through the 1980s, socialism was popular in the Third World, and most developing countries owned their key industries such as telecommunications, oil and gas, power, and transport. These sectors were off-limits to foreigners. In fact, many emerging markets saw Western investment in the these industries as colonialism; thus, in Mexico, for example, the date the government nationalized the oil industry (in 1938) is practically a national holiday. The 1990s saw many of these sectors privatized—with Western firms being reluctantly invited in—but suspicions against multinationals linger from the socialist days, even as privatization improves service.

In Guyana, for example, ordinary individuals waited one to two years for the government-owned phone company to install a new line. Now, with Atlantic Tele-Network managing the system, installation time is down to two months, yet the company still faces frivolous lawsuits from the government and it agencies.

Taher Gargour, a securities analyst at HSBC Securities in Egypt, summarizes a common theme, "The government and the public are still divided over privatization. They're afraid it means the end of the welfare state and guaranteed employment. It's a reactionary attitude to the global economy."

WHEN DO THE BARRIERS CRUMBLE?

What factors enable foreigners to circumvent the entrenched obstacles to entry? For starters, local business people realize that increasing their own wealth requires additional investment, and the local economy can only partially fulfill this need. The preferred vehicle for gaining more capital is borrowing from local banks, but at some point the lenders want a corresponding equity buildup. Given the limitations of domestic equity sources, the local operators invite foreign equity capital. The sponsors of a luxury hotel in Warsaw, for example, found Polish equity capital and bank loans, but they needed foreign partners to fill a $20 million funding gap.

The locals may desire access to Western technology and managerial skills. At first, they seek to obtain these resources through licensing agreements or consulting contracts with multinationals. Such arrangements involve no new foreign capital. Sacrificing local ownership becomes necessary when pursuing these half measures is unsuccessful. This course of action is taken reluctantly, and its implementation is often delayed until an industry's backwardness affects an economy's well-being. In Indonesia, the country suffered repeated brownouts and electricity shortages in the early 1990s, and Jakarta businesses lost money as a result. Eventually, the government allowed

Western power producers to participate in electricity production as owners. In Costa Rica, local businessmen signed up with Millicom International Cellular, a European telecommunications firm, to start up the country's first cellular phone franchise. Sometimes, when a new technology requires a rapid learning curve, home-country businesses seek a foreign partner to gain "first mover" status.

The local establishment also drops entry barriers when there is a pent-up demand for Western products and services. Whether this demand is from businesses or consumers, pressure builds and the foreigners are allowed in. Initial steps, such as a local firm handling import sales, evolve into joint ventures and greenfield investments. For example, McDonald's, the fast-food purveyor, operates in dozens of developing countries. Merrill Lynch sells its investment banking services through foreign offices, and Nokia distributes its phones on a global basis.

Emerging markets are dependent on selling their products into Western economies. A *quid pro quo* for this access is opening portions of their domestic markets to multinationals. This availability is provided grudgingly, and developing countries routinely ignore their responsibilities under "free trade" treaties with the West.

For example, in June 2000 the U.S. Trade Department complained that South Korea refused to honor its agreements to import U.S. cars and foodstuffs, while furiously expanding the exports of Korean cars. In 1999, U.S. and European firms sold a miniscule 2,401 cars to Korea's 47 million people, but in that same year, Korea's car exports were 1.5 million. In Malaysia, counterfeit compact disc factories operate with little government interference and pay no royalties to the Western record companies whose products they copy. Nepal movie theatres routinely show bootleg American films.

The trade system between the West and the Third World is far from perfect. The treaties provide a wedge for the multinationals to gain a foothold, but follow-through is difficult. The business climate for foreigners is thus shrouded in ambivalence. In an ideal situation, the locals prefer to live without foreign ownership. In the real world, however, they need Western money, technology, and products. How they gain access to these items is problematic. At the top of the preference list are "noncontrol relationships" such as Western loans, license agreements, and passive equity investments. At the bottom of the list is the outright acquisition of a domestic firm by a transnational.

A special category of foreign investment is the 100 percent export platform. In this type of enterprise, local resources and local labor produce goods that are sold outside of the country; thus, the business doesn't interfere with home country oligopolies. Textile plants in Pakistan and gas liquification facilities in Indonesia are prime illustrations of successful export platforms.

OLIGOPOLIES

The economies of emerging markets feature oligopolies that dominate the principal industrial sectors. Mexico, where I have closed many corporate finance deals, is typical. Two companies control the beer industry, two companies control the cigarette business, two companies own 86 percent of the cement industry, and one firm has 90 percent of the bread market. A nexus of elite family tradition, political protection, and foreign corporate exclusion preserves these profitable oligopolies, which form the base from which the wealthy families spring into new industries such as cable-TV and cellular phones. Few major projects go ahead without the participation of these groups, and it is *de rigueur* for multinationals to ally themselves with such families before entering.

BUSINESS LAW

Legal documentation in the emerging markets follows a format that is similar to the Western variety. Contracts tend to be shorter and less dense than in a developed country, but the process of negotiating fine points with business people and lawyers is about the same. Contracts involving Westerners are usually drafted in English. Unless a special need arises, the document is not translated into the local language.

Emerging market legal systems are poor venues in which to settle business disputes. Court calendars are crowded and hearings are postponed interminably. Judges are subject to undue influence by local enterprises and attorneys, and they are sometimes open to under-the-table payments for ruling in one party's favor. Even if a foreigner wins a lawsuit, enforcing the judgment is problematic. Local authorities may refuse to liquidate or attach the defendant's assets. Arbitration and negotiation are the suggested ways to remedy a contractual matter.

INTELLECTUAL PROPERTY RIGHTS

Most emerging markets have regulations that protect intellectual property rights, but the laws are loosely enforced. As a result, patent-protected drugs made by Merck and Pfizer, for example, are manufactured in many developing nations without the payment of royalties. Laboratories in Argentina, for example, pirate about $500 million annually from multinationals, according to Pharmaceutical Research and Manufacturers of America, a trade group. Similarly, the copying of Western books, compact discs, and videos is a large business in Southeast Asia, with the counterfeiter making no payments to the owners of the copyrights. These problems attract attention from the local authorities, since foreign firms protest, but results are slow.

PHYSICAL INFRASTRUCTURE

The physical infrastructure of an emerging market bears a direct relation to its per capita GNP level. Upper income countries (per capita GNP more than $3,000) have the basic transport, telecommunications, and power services. The road, air, and rail network is in good condition, the telephones work, and power generation is reliable. Infrastructure performance is worse in the mid-income and lower-income countries, particularly as you move out of the large cities. Roads may be clogged with traffic and in poor repair, phone and fax machines may work only intermittently, and mail is not delivered. Power grids "brownout" during peak times, or simply shut down on a regular basis. To remedy this last situation, every tourist hotel in the Dominican Republic has a back-up generator.

The construction of a quality physical infrastructure is hampered by several factors. One, infrastructure is capital-intensive and the Third World lacks long-term capital. Two, the infrastructure sector was dominated by parastatals for many years; they were reluctant to raise electricity and phone rates for political reasons, thus cutting themselves off from the funds needed to maintain service. And three, infrastructure projects don't generate "hard currency." This fact, coupled with the currency devaluation risk, restricts foreign interest in the sector, despite the strong local demand for the products or service. In Cameroon, for example, a poor African nation with a per capita GNP of only $620, the new cellular phone company expects demand for its phones to climb from zero to 100,000 in the first eight months of its franchise. Even then, this country will have only 11 phones per 1,000 people, versus 644 per 1,000 in the United States.

The plant and equipment of the private sector is often run down. Expensive long-term capital encourages businesses to defer investment, while the monopoly structure of industry allows operators to make money even with antiquated machinery. Third World factories are frequently ramshackle affairs that are in serious need of maintenance and repair.

SOCIAL SERVICES

The healthcare industry in an emerging market is typically run by the government. Service levels are a far cry from Western standards.

Private institutions that cater to wealthy clients supplement government hospitals.

Education is a terribly undeveloped resource in the Third World. Many children, particularly girls, stop formal education in grade school so they can work on the family farm or in factories. In India, only half of the population can read and write. Higher education, such as high school and college, is often free-of-charge but enrollment space is very limited, and the facilities lack equipment that their Western counterparts consider a necessity. And finally, emerging market countries don't offer the lavish social welfare and retirement schemes provided by Japan, the United States, and Germany, because they can't afford them. Unemployed citizens and retirees rely on family and friends during hard times.

WORKFORCE

A common generalization by Westerners is that the emerging market workforce has a poor work ethic. My experience leans toward the opposite conclusion, as many middle managers and factory workers put in long days and long commutes. Their productivity is low because their capital equipment and training are spotty by Western standards. Plus, the employees are not highly motivated. The large family firms don't offer stock option programs, and the recently privatized state concerns are still shaking the civil service mentality. Labor is cheap in these countries, and companies frequently underemploy workers to avoid investment in labor-saving machinery. This gives the impression that an employee is not working hard enough.

Moonlighting is a common practice in emerging markets. The head of household who occupies a low-level position may work two jobs to sustain a decent standard of living. Workers eligible for factory jobs are poorly educated and only semi-literate. Their ability to operate sophisticated machinery and personal computers is thus dependent on vocational training provided by the employer.

Developing nations have a shortage of lawyers, accountants, and technical personnel that are qualified by international standards. Local practitioners are capable of achieving these standards but they must receive training and experience. Unfortunately, this doesn't happen as often as it should. Ambitious people see opportunities in the West, receive the requisite skills, and don't return to the home country. At the World Bank, I met dozens of Third World people with advanced financial training. Few of them wanted to go back to living in a poor country. Washington, DC was more comfortable and interesting than a Third World city.

MARKET RESEARCH AND GOVERNMENT STATISTICS

Western firms like to conduct detailed studies before investing in a new market. In developing nations, however, trade associations and government offices that prepare operating statistics either don't exist or lack the resources to track industries properly. The Western firm, therefore, commits on less-than-complete information. When I worked at the $1.8 billion Asian private equity fund, the unavoidable holes in my deal summaries would drive one of the sponsors, Edison International, up a wall. Edison's conservative U.S. management wanted all the I's dotted and all the T's crossed. It was hard for me to explain that doing business in Sumatra was different than closing a deal in Arizona.

In 1998, I completed a $43 million equity investment in a South Korean paper manufacturer. The firm exported heavily to Mainland China. Working with international paper consultants, I tried to learn about the supply and demand dynamics of paper in China. Accurate statistics weren't available, and we pieced together a forecast from sundry bits of information that would have never made the grade in a U.S. context.

Official macroeconomic reports cover information on balance of payments, foreign debt, money supply, and foreign exchange reserves, among other items. The reliability of these reports varies widely among countries, as they are not audited by independent professionals. Tardiness is also a problem, as investors don't get this data on a timely basis.

SUPPLY AND DISTRIBUTION SYSTEMS

Supply and distribution systems fall below minimum Western standards in the emerging markets. Besides the limited transportation infrastructure, countries lack storage facilities and logistical networks. In Russia, for example, up to one-fourth of the grain harvest routinely spoils before delivery to the consumer, due to warehouse shortages and poor transport coordination.

International companies considering a local presence must confirm that supplies made locally (1) meet Western quality standards and (2) are deliverable on a timely basis. In Russia, McDonald's trained its suppliers in quality control and on-time delivery. Local suppliers were neither accustomed to the significance of customer service nor to the importance of product standardization. This situation is not uncommon. Centrally planned economies and capitalist oligopolies left little room for true competition, so product suppliers became lax. The lesson for the multinational is to secure supply sources before commencing local production. Otherwise, be prepared to import raw materials and semi-finished goods for a manufacturing facility.

BANKING SYSTEMS

Local banks tend to be unsophisticated and subject to undue political influence. Short-term financing and everyday cash management are handled well, but the loan extension process is a throwback to the United States in the 1950s. Loan officers have little credit training and insist on loans that are secured by "hard assets" and personal guarantees. Asset appraisals in the Third World are subject to exaggeration, and enforcing a personal guarantee is difficult. The concept of project finance and "cash flow" financing is still in its infancy, so international players should be prepared to provide a local venture with a solid equity base and a parent guarantee of its debt.

In many countries, the commercial banks function as an extension of the Finance Ministry. At the behest of the government, they place loans to industrial sectors slated for development, with little regard for credit quality. The banks are easy "loan windows" for prominent backers of the governing parties, and monies are provided for questionable projects that wouldn't hold up under commercial scrutiny.

The derivative negative effects of substandard banking practices play a role in every financial crisis. After the 1997 devaluation, about 60 percent of the commercial loans in Thailand's banking system were "nonperforming," thus ensuring a freeze on economic activity. Many of these loans were made to real estate projects with superficially strong loan-to-asset value ratios. In South Korea, bad loan portfolios topped $40 billion in 2000. Earlier, the government had pushed banks into financing sectors with capacity gluts, and the additional product didn't find buyers.

In Eastern European, African, and Central Asian countries, the banking systems are less capable than those in Latin America and Southeast Asia. In some cases, they lack sufficient hard currency to support trade requirements. Western firms use countertrade methods such as barter, counter-purchase, switch, or buyback.

CURRENCY REGIME

As mentioned earlier, one of the biggest deterrents to emerging market investing is the unstable currency regime. A Western firm can place $10 million into a local business and, overnight, a devaluation can decrease the investment's value by 30 percent to 40 percent. Despite policy makers' and pundits' promises that "it won't happen again," devaluations are a recurring phenomenon.

The principal emerging markets operate reasonably open currency regimes. Sizable amounts of local currency can be exchanged into hard currencies. Others, such as Iran and Russia, operate dual systems whereby certain monies can be exchanged freely, while other amounts must be changed over time, subject to government approval. The most restrictive system involves official permission for all monies over a fixed number, such as $10,000 U.S. equivalent. The latter system typically involves a queue, where Westerners wait in line for hard currency as it becomes available at the central bank.

The pernicious history of devaluation underlies the lack of long-term bond, fixed-rate markets in the Third World. Who wants to buy a 10-year obligation that can halve in value in a few years? As I noted earlier, devaluation expectations encourage the average citizen to keep savings in tangible objects, such as gold jewelry, rather than in local banks or mutual funds. Adjustable-rate debts are the norm, along with short maturities. This makes life tougher for business, which then has trouble predicting interest costs.

TARIFFS AND IMPORT LICENSES

Emerging market tariffs remain high, especially for imported goods that are produced locally. Tariffs serve three key objectives: (1) they protect local companies that make similar products; (2) by curtailing demand for imports, they save foreign exchange; and (3) they raise money for the government.

Other barriers to foreign entry are import-licensing regimes and quotas. Here, a government agency allocates the ability to import selected products into the country.

GETTING TO KNOW A PARTNER

Most Westerners discover that the investment process takes more time than in a developed nation. Personal relationships and "getting to know" a business partner count for more than in the West. Negotiations proceed cautiously. The bureaucratic and legal machinery for closing a transaction do not carry the sense of urgency found in wealthier nations. For a first-time entrant to the emerging market, the pace may seem agonizing slow. My advice is "Get used to it." You're not going to change things overnight.

The emphasis on personal connections stems from the weak legal systems in these countries. Disputes are difficult to settle legally and can wind-up in the courts for years. By doing business with friends, local businesspeople believe that the inevitable disputes in a business arrangement can be settled in a friendly manner (see Figure 3.2). Personal trust is thus a substitute for the phalanx of lawyers common to U.S. commercial disputes.

CULT OF THE CHAIRMAN

Emerging market business is characterized by a continuous reliance and belief in personal ties, rather than professional relationships. This phenomenon is most prevalent at the family firms that domi-

Source: Corbis Images/Picture Quest.

FIGURE 3.2   Be prepared to socialize with people of varied cultures. Be sensitive to the many differences.

nate much of the developing economies, but it is also prominent at broadly-held public companies. The patriarch—or the chairman/potentate—is considered all knowing within the firm, and this obeisance ties the hands of management and shareholders. New ideas and constructive criticisms are caught-up in what the chairman says or thinks, and only his contacts can instill a sense of change. Over the long-term, this situation hurts efficiencies and wealth creation.

In South Korea, the government was trying to reform the economy's largest groups, by breaking them up, but several chairmen resisted. In one case, Chung Ju Yung, chairman of Hyundai Group, blocked the government's efforts to spin-out Hyundai Motor, the conglomerate's auto-making arm. At age 84, when most businessmen have retired to golf and bridge, Mr. Yung still commanded the loyalty of managers and retained informal control over corporate actions at many affiliates. Attempts by the government to water down his influence got nowhere.

In one Indian joint venture, the American partner wanted to liquidate the sizeable operation. With sale proceeds of the deal estimated at $1 billion, the U.S. firm wanted to hire an investment bank to "shop" the business on a global basis, but the local partner's executives resisted. "Our chairman knows all the potential buyers," they insisted, but the U.S. managers argued for a transaction handled in a professional way, that maximized dollars.

EXECUTIVES PLAYING DUMB

In negotiating a deal with an emerging market executive, the Western manager should be prepared for the "playing dumb" act. The local executive will be blissfully unaware of Western business conventions when it's in his interest to be forgetful. He may say things like "That's never done in Poland" or "No Polish company would ever agree to that." Generally, these assertions are not supported by fact, and the hapless Western investor is reduced to disproving a negative.

At the same time, the local executive may have a good command of the most arcane Western terminology when it supports his position. In one of my South Korean deals, the company displayed a seeming ignorance regarding most aspects of U.S.-style convertible bonds. However, when I tried to slip-in an anti-dilution provision that was favorable to the investors, the chairman spotted it immediately. Days of lengthy discussion followed to resolve the matter.

MANUFACTURING ORIENTATION

The industrialized portion of the developing economies are manufacturing oriented, and the sizeable businesses there involve lots of bricks and mortar. Service, software, and intellectual-content businesses, until recently, were not considered storehouses of value by local groups, and they devoted little attention to them. Similarly, banks and financial institutions refused to lend significant monies to these service sectors.

The inability of these economies to place a value on services and intellectual property hinders the locals' ability to find investment funds for these areas. So, while services are the engine behind the U.S. economy, the Third World economy lags seriously behind.

SUMMARY

Emerging markets are typified by oligopolies and high trade barriers. Local businessmen are extremely concerned about large foreign companies buying up local industries, which are often uncompetitive internationally.

The Western company used to doing business in nations with a strong rule-of-law, a solid physical infrastructure, and a stable currency regime needs to adjust its game plan before entering a developing country. Recruiting a respected local partner is the best way to start.

CHAPTER 4

What Attracts Multinational Firms to the Emerging Markets?

Multinational companies are attracted to the emerging markets for two reasons: (1) they perceive these nations as having growth opportunities that are superior to their home countries; and (2) they can use these countries as low-cost production platforms for goods sold to First World customers.

THE IMPORTANCE OF GROWTH

Sustained growth of sales and earnings is vital to the survival of a corporation. Without it, a business withers on the vine. Ambitious employees leave to join expanding firms with advancement potential, while financing sources, particularly equity investors, desert the business for companies that offer higher returns. With unmotivated employees and disinterested investors, the no-growth company has a dismal future. If it's publicly traded, the firm is takeover bait for an aggressive operator. Renato Soru, Chief Executive of Italy's Tiscali, Spa, puts it succinctly, "You either expand or you'll die."

Growth Perception versus Reality

Developing country economies, on an aggregate basis, grow faster than the wealthy nations, but the difference is not as great as media outlets would have you believe. The growth premium of emerging markets vis-à-vis the First World was less than 1 percent over the 1981–1998 time period (see Table 4.1). World Bank projections for Third World growth over 2002–2008 suggest a greater divergence, but this optimism must be taken with a grain of salt. The Bank has been notoriously bad at predicting the crises that afflict these regions, which then subvert the Bank's projections.

The developed economies tend to grow at a measured pace, with five or six years of 2 percent to 3 percent annual growth, which is then interrupted by a brief recession. Activity then declines by 0.5 percent to 1 percent for a year or so. In contrast, emerging economies show inconsistent behavior that belies the conventional portrait of upward progress.

For example, in the 1980s, Latin America moved backwards in per capita GNP income, as debt crises and continued devaluations crippled economies for practically a decade. The recovery years were then slowed by currency crises in Mexico (1994) and Brazil (1998). In Asia, the Tigers (Indonesia, Malaysia, Philippines, South Korea, and Thailand) consistently grew by 6 percent (or more annually) only to face severe recessions in the late 1990s. Economic bouncebacks can be rapid, however, as evidenced by South Korea's 1999 GNP gain of 10 percent, coming off a crushing recession when economic activity declined by 6 percent.

TABLE 4.1 World Economic Growth, 1981–2008 (Annual Percentage Change in Real GDP)

	Historical		Forecast
	1981–1990	**1991–1998**	**2002–2008**
OECD countries	3.0	2.2	2.6
Developing countries	3.3	3.2	4.9
Difference	+0.3	+1.0	+2.3

Source: The World Bank, *Global Economic Prospects,* 2001.

The Excitement over Real Growth

What's exciting about entering these markets? One attraction is how specific sectors explode when new products are introduced. In the United States, cable-television subscriber increases are 1 percent to 2 percent per year, equal to population growth, since the customer base is totally saturated. In contrast, cable television in Brazil is a novel service and demand is strong. From 1997 to 2000, the Brazilian subscriber base tripled, and Kagan's World Media predicts another tripling by 2003.

International Data Corporation predicts Mexican Internet use will rise sevenfold by 2004, and Bell South's wireless customer base in Latin America doubled from 1998 to 1999. Spending $3 billion to build its Latin American business, the company estimates it is now valued at $14 billion.

Growth and Stockholder Value

The principal motive for running a business is increasing shareholder value. History shows that a strong growth record provides a good stock price, so executives have every incentive to expand their businesses. High-growth companies receive higher P/E ratios—and thus higher prices—than low-growth counterparts (see Table 4.2).

As Table 4.2 indicates, a "high-growth" company can earn the same earnings per share (EPS) as a low-growth concern, but its stock price will be higher, as investors multiply EPS by a larger P/E ratio.

BASIC PRINCIPLES OF CORPORATE VALUATION

To fully understand growth's impact on a company's stock value, the reader should consider the basic principles of corporate valuation.

TABLE 4.2   Growth and P/E Ratios

	Growth Rate (%)	P/E Ratio at June 2000
High-growth companies		
Cisco Systems	50	160
Microsoft	30	49
Scientific Atlanta	35	52
Low-growth companies		
Ford Motor	9	8
Maytag	7	10
Sears	12	9

Investors apply two approaches to value an ongoing business: intrinsic value and relative value. They are summarized as follows:

1. *Intrinsic value:* A business equals the net present value of its dividends. Intrinsic value is sometimes called "fundamental value" or the "discounted cash flow" technique.
2. *Relative value:* A firm's value is determined by comparing it to similar companies' values. If General Motors is trading at 15 times earnings, all things being equal, then Ford Motor should trade at 15 times earnings.

Starting with Intrinsic Value

A stock's intrinsic value is the present value of its stream of future cash dividends. This value is calculated with different formulas, depending on the situation at hand. The simplest formula is used for firms that have a stable capital structure and growth rate:

Discounted Cash Dividend Valuation Approach:
Constant Growth Model

$$P = \frac{D_1}{k - g}$$

where P = Intrinsic value (i.e., correct price)

D_1 = Next year's cash dividend

k = Annual rate of return required by shareholders

g = Expected annual growth rate of dividends

To calculate the intrinsic value, the practitioner plugs in the variables D_1, k, and g. He derives D_1, and g from his financial projections. We discuss k later in the chapter.

For companies that are not expected to have anything approaching a constant growth rate, such as a cyclical business, a start-up venture, or a firm with a history of special dividends and spin-offs, the formula is modified. The practice is to predict dividends for a 5- to 10-year period, after which time the company pays out dividends in a constant fashion. A 10-year time horizon is shown next:

Discounted Cash Dividend Valuation Approach:
Two-Step Growth Model

Step 1: Variable growth rates (years 1 to 10)
Step 2: Constant growth rate (year 11)

$$P = \frac{D_0(1+g_1)}{(1+k)^1} + \frac{D_1(1+g_2)}{(1+k)^2} + K + \frac{D_9(1+g_{10})}{(1+k)^{10}} + \frac{\dfrac{D_{10}(1+g_{11})}{k-g}}{(1+k)^{10}}$$

where P = Intrinsic value

D = Current year's dividend

k = Annual rate of return required by shareholders

g = Yearly growth rate

g_{11} = Constant growth rate after year 10

In the two-step model, g_1 is the growth rate of the dividend in year one, g_2 in year two, and so on until year 11 when the model becomes steady state. Alternative dividend models value stocks that don't pay dividends, consider situations involving short-term periods, and allow for periods of varying growth and discount rates.

Under any scenario, a higher growth rate produces an improved stock value. Consider the fictitious Metal Bender Corp. (MBC):

Metal Bender Corp. (MBC) Common Stock

Compound annual dividend growth	8.0%
Next year's dividend rate	$1.50
Expected constant dividend growth rate (g)	8.0%
Dividend payout ratio	50.0%
Earnings per share	$3.00
Compound annual earnings per share growth	8.0%
MBC stockholder's required annual rate of return (k), given a choice of alternative investments	11.0%

Using this information, an investor applies the dividend discount formula to derive a $50 share value:

$$\text{MBC price} = \frac{D_1}{k-g}$$

$$= \frac{\$1.50}{.11-.08} = \$50.00$$

Suppose MBC enters an emerging market, is successful there, and increases its growth rate to 9 percent. In this instance, the stock price jumps to $75.00:

$$\text{MBC price} = \frac{D_1}{k-g}$$

$$= \frac{\$1.50}{.11-.09} = \$75.00$$

Thus, even a 1 percent change in MBC's growth rate produces a 50 percent boost to the stock price.

The trick for public firms venturing into the emerging markets is to (a) balance the perception of higher growth against (b) the perception of higher risk (see Figure 4.1). If Wall Street sees a 1 percent added risk (higher k) to an emerging markets entry, the impact of improving growth is canceled out, as illustrated below:

9% growth cancelled out by 12% capital cost

$$\text{MBC price} = \frac{D_1}{k-g}$$

$$= \frac{\$1.50}{.12 - .09} = \$50.00$$

Here, the stock price remains at $50, even though the growth rate increases.

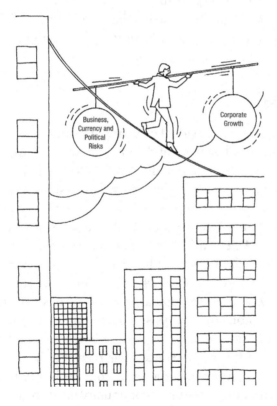

FIGURE 4.1   The emerging market balancing act.

TABLE 4.3   P/E Ratios of Similar Businesses

	P/E
Duke Energy	18
Southern Company	14
Electric Utility Average	12

Note: P/E's calculated at August 2000.

Duke Energy and Southern Company are two firms that play the balancing act well. Stuck in low-growth electric utility businesses in the United States, they made significant commitments to the emerging markets. Earnings growth accompanied these actions, as did higher risks, but Wall Street de-emphasized the potential problems. The firms have the premium P/E ratios when compared to similar businesses (see Table 4.3).

Relative Value

The use of k and g as individual company statistics independent of the broader market is a key tenet of the intrinsic value crowd, but the difficulty of forecasting corporate dividends and determining the appropriate discount rate spawns arguments. Discussions among intrinsic value investors involve comments such as "How can you assign an 11 percent growth rate to the stock's dividends when the historical growth rate is 14 percent?" "How can our estimates of g equals 12 percent and k equals 17 be correct; they indicate a \$14 stock price when the market price is \$24. Our numbers must be wrong!"

Although k and g are popular subjects in business schools, the inability of investors and analysts to agree on exact estimates for individual stocks, and the huge price differences created by small differences in these statistics, reduce their relevance in the real world. While believing that the intrinsic value concept is intuitively correct, a large portion of the investment community abandons it as unworkable from a practical point of view. In its stead, analysts rely on the "relative value" concept, which uses comparisons as the basis for establishing prices. The theory is simple enough. If they participate in the same industry, companies with comparable track records and balance sheets should have comparable valuation yardsticks. Since k and g statistics are indeterminate, the relative value school adopts substitute measures, the most popular being the P/E ratio.

Relative value adherents can be spotted when they are saying something like "Merck's stock is undervalued at a 19 P/E ratio, yet it is growing faster than Eli Lilly, which has a 22 P/E ratio" or "Union Carbide is overvalued. Its 20 P/E is 33 percent higher than the industry's 15 P/E ratio, but its projected growth is only 14 percent higher than the industry's."

Relative value investors employ other financial statistics. Ratios such as the Enterprise Value to Earnings before Interest, Taxes, Depreciation, and Amortization (EBITDA), Share Price to Book Value, and Enterprise Value to Sales are popular. Many industry-specific ratios exist. For example, oil analysts use Share Price to Number of Barrels per Share as one barometer of relative value. Cable television analysts use the Share Price to Number of Connected Homes per Share; Cement analysts, Tons of Production Capacity per Share, and so on. The P/E ratio, however, remains the most popular statistic.

Wall Street synthesizes the k and g variables of the dividend discount into, the P/E ratio. Business publications constantly print statements such as "Philip Morris is trading at a 16 P/E, 10 percent over the market average," "Dow Chemical looks cheap at a 15 P/E." Individual ratios are expressed in relative terms. When a firm's P/E ratio exceeds the P/E ratio of the stock market as a whole, that company is considered to have growth potential exceeding the prospects of the average listed company. Conversely, a relatively low P/E indicates a profile that is below average. Analysts extend these comparisons to a firm's peers.

Changes in the perception of a stock's risk or growth characteristics alter the P/E ratio. The P/E ratio climbs when investors boost a stock's indicated growth rate. Likewise, the P/E ratio decreases with a rise in the perception of a stock's risk. This having been said, equity investors focus on growth rates far more than perceived risks, which is why Wall Street usually welcomes companies into the emerging markets.

THE PRICE OF RISK

A stock's required rate of return is based on a relative analysis of the returns being offered by competing investments, taking into account the respective risks involved. Investments perceived as risky because of checkered track records or questionable prospects should provide investors with a higher rate of return. Figure 4.2 illustrates a risk/return matrix in graphic form.

The logic of the matrix is simple. Unpredictability and volatility in investment returns are bad. Stability and assurance of returns are

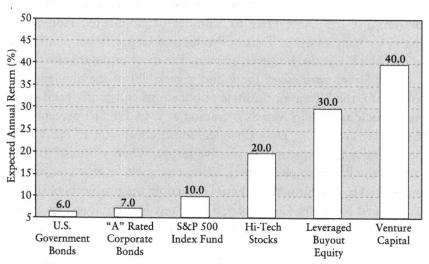

Note: Riskier investments require higher expected returns. Multinationals seek equity returns of 20% to 25% in the emerging markets.

FIGURE 4.2   Risk and return graph for November 2000.

good. The required return of any stock should equal the rate of return on a relatively riskless investment, such as a U.S. government bond, plus a premium for the added risk incurred by the investor for holding a nongovernment-guaranteed investment. The premium goes up as the investment becomes more risky. In my experience, multinational corporations and institutional investors require expected returns of 20 percent to 25 percent (in US$) on emerging market equity investments. Haidje Rustau, Asian equity analyst at Morgan Stanley Dean Witter, says that his firm's minimum IRR requirement on emerging market stocks is the US$ yield on the country's sovereign bond plus 5 percent. Thus, when the government of Hungary bond yields 8.60 percent, the minimum IRR for Hungarian equities should be 13.60 percent in US$ terms. These various yardsticks place the perceived risks and expected IRR's between high-tech stocks and leveraged buyouts.

DEFINING GROWTH OPPORTUNITIES

Opportunities to exploit an emerging market's economic growth manifest themselves in several ways:

1. Rapid rise in GNP.
2. New product introduction.
3. Market share expansion throughout management expertise and abundant capital resources.
4. Consolidation of smaller firms to form a major company.

Rapid Rise in GNP

As an emerging market's per capita GNP rises faster than a developed country's, the sales for the products and services associated with higher GNP climbs rapidly. In essence, a rising tide lifts all boats. Even the demand for mundane products jumps. For example, from

TABLE 4.4   Computer Use and Country GNP

Personal Computers per 1,000 People	Average GNP per Capita ($)
Less than 5	430
5–20	990
20–50	3,880
50–150	14,680
150 or more	27,570

1997–2000, the amount of paper sold in Eastern Europe grew by 10 percent annually, versus a 5 percent rate in Western Europe. In South Korea, annual sales of cement climbed by 9 percent annually in the mid 1990s, when the U.S. rise was only 3 percent annually. In China, electricity-consumption climbs 9 percent per year when the comparable figure in Japan is 2 percent. That's why Western power, cement, and paper firms spend billions of dollars in overseas expansion.

Wealth brings a need for products and services that U.S. citizens take for granted. A personal computer is a common appliance in a U.S. household, and its use is highly correlated to GNP levels (see Table 4.4). Richer countries use far more PC's than poor nations.

New Product Introduction

Developing countries are attractive secondary markets for companies offering a classic growth product, which is a product that no one (or corporation) knew they needed before the product's invention. A typical product is introduced first in the developing world, where it gains acceptance, and then it is sold through to the emerging markets. Such items are frequently the result of technological innovations (e.g., cellular phones and Internet service). AOL, for example, made its big push into Latin America after success in the United States and Europe. Susan Segal who handles emerging market deals at Chase Capital Partners, supports developing country firms that imitate U.S. ventures. "We are not going to finance unrecognizable models," she says.

In other instances, a traditional, low-tech offering from the First World makes a big splash. After Pizza Hut entered El Salvador in 1989, the company's franchises multiplied quickly. The fast-food chain now has 32 locations in this small country.

Market Share Expansion

Emerging markets have relatively mature industries, such as packaged food, beer and tobacco. The local players usually enjoy an oligopoly and become complacent. Product quality is generally not up to Western standards. Assuming a foreign firm gains entry, the inefficiency, backwardness, and capital constraints of the homegrown industry make it easy pickings. A multinational's sizeable balance sheet, its modern production, distribution and marketing techniques, and its sophisticated management team are powerful weapons against the local players.

Sometimes, the multinational's management skills are not the impetus for attracting market share. Rather, its ability to fund huge capital investments is the driving force. In Argentina, for example, local broadband Internet service providers team up with a foreign partner. The latter supplies the massive amount of capital needed to set up a wireless system, and the former provides the customers, contacts and licenses. Velcom, the U.S. broadband firm, promised to invest $300 million in its partner, an amount the Argentine firm could never have raised on its own.

When a government sells a state-owned enterprise to foreigners, it seeks both management assistance and capital for supporting the business on a forward basis. In selling a 40 percent interest in its phone company to GTE for $1 billion, Venezuela wanted the firm to benefit from GTE's managerial expertise, as well as its ability to assist in the funding of hundreds of thousands of new phone lines.

Consolidation

Merger and acquisition activity is much less than in the Western nations, even after accounting for lower GNP levels. Fragmented "Mom & Pop" industries that have long been "rolled up" in the United States are consolidation opportunities for sophisticated foreign buyers. In South America, Hicks Muse, an $8 billion investment firm, is crafting a sports conglomerate through acquisition. At the same time, it introduces concepts that are new to Latin sports, like logo merchandising, luxury boxes, and corporate sponsorship. In Bolivia, Canada's Multivision consolidated small cable-television operators to form a national firm.

Foreigners have a major advantage in the consolidation game. The local players lack transaction experience, and they consider acquisitions in an unsophisticated way, focusing on the "hard asset" value of a business rather than its future cash flow. This way of thinking is an impediment to acquisitive dealmaking. Knowledgeable sellers insist on prices in excess of historical cost, believing a premium compensates them for the "goodwill" of a successful firm. When buyers don't meet the sellers halfway, transactions don't happen.

PARTICIPATING IN EMERGING MARKET GROWTH

Like developed nations, the emerging markets offer a number of options for establishing an operating presence. These range from licensing arrangements, where the multinational's in-country role is minimal, to the full-scale acquisition of an ongoing business, which involves substantial capital and management resources. A lower commitment level has a distinct appeal for a company that is unsure of a new market, or one that doesn't want to risk the capital that growth requires.

These half measures permit the would-be entrant to "get its feet wet" in a country; however, there are drawbacks. The main issue is a lack of control, a critical obstacle for many multinationals.

TABLE 4.5 Entry Strategies for Multinationals in Emerging Markets

Strategy	Primary Advantages	Primary Disadvantages
1. Licensing Western products to locals	■ Near zero capital investment ■ Extend brand to new market ■ Cheap means of accessing developing nation	■ Very poor control elements ■ Risk theft of technology and processes ■ Difficult to verify sales audit
2. Export	■ Near zero capital investment ■ Local agents handle many details	■ High tariffs keep out imports, complicating this tactic ■ Non-official barriers discourage non-essential exports into their country
3. Franchising	■ Capital usually provided by franchisee ■ Rapid expansion potential	■ Application limited to a few industries (restaurants, retailing, some services) ■ Limited control over franchises; reputation can suffer ■ "Model" must be adapted to local tastes
4. Marketing and distribution alliances	■ Capital investment needs reduced in comparison to alternatives 5, 6, 7, and 8 ■ Cheap means of accessing new markets ■ Often cancelable with few penalties	■ Limited control ability ■ Risk of third-party theft of product knowledge or technology

(continued)

TABLE 4.5 (Continued)

Strategy	Primary Advantages	Primary Disadvantages
5. Joint Venture	■ Share expenses ■ Learning experience ■ Partner has local know-how and contacts	■ Share control and profits ■ Theft of multinational's core competencies by locals ■ Agree on mutual exit strategy upfront
6. "Greenfield" start-up in local market	■ 100% control ■ Modern processes and outlook	■ Suicidal tactic without a local partner ■ High failure rate ■ Larger companies are not entrepreneurial enough to ensure success
7. Acquisition	■ Acceptable if local interest is meaningful. ■ Majority control ■ Instant market share and infrastructure	■ The acquired company may have hidden liabilities that were not uncovered by due diligence ■ Strict labor laws limit U.S. style layoffs and restructurings ■ You're often buying market share rather than modern production/service facilities. Lots of follow-on investment needed
8. Privatization	Similar to acquisition	■ Governments are difficult to deal with ■ Continued government ownership/involvement can be a requirement ■ Not many good deals left ■ Otherwise, similar to an acquisition

Nonacquisition arrangements involve management groups that are not 100 percent beholden to the multinational. Summary advantages and disadvantages of entry strategies are presented in Table 4.5.

USE LOCAL CONTACTS

Whatever tactic a foreigner decides on, it's important that he looks for a good local player to work with. The best way to begin this search is to canvass multinational firms that are already active in the country, and ask their managers for ideas, contacts and reference checks. In addition to foreign operating companies, international law firms, accounting firms, and commercial banks usually have local alliances, and the multilateral investment organizations and U.S. embassies can provide related information. Avoid government development arms and local chambers of commerce. They are unsophisticated and understaffed; they aren't good resources for this type of search.

JOINT VENTURE

A joint venture is an excellent second-stage entry tactic for an international firm with an established sales presence, and many prominent firms use them (see Figure 4.3). After selling product in China

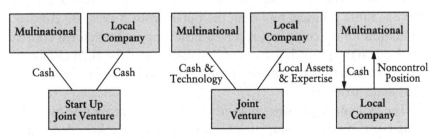

FIGURE 4.3 Joint venture forms.

for several years, General Motors set up a manufacturing joint venture with Shanghai Automotive. A joint venture can take several forms. Both parties can contribute cash to form a start-up. One can contribute technology and cash, while the other puts up operating assets and local expertise, or the multinational can acquire newly issued stock of the local firm. The third option requires intense due diligence because emerging market firms tend to have hidden liabilities, ranging from social-service obligations for thousands of employees to environmental problems that date back many years.

Since a joint venture suggests a significant financial commitment and a major "on-the-ground" presence for the foreigner, it implies careful study. With the assistance of a strong local partner, getting your money into a country should be easy, but problems arise when you want to "cash out" of the deal. In addition to the voluminous regulations on foreign entry, most emerging markets impose restrictions on how fast foreigner firms can liquidate their long-term holdings. Large joint ventures might want to custom-tailor their exit arrangements with the government.

The foreigner's exit mechanism must also be carefully negotiated with the local operator. The legal documentation should be very detailed, with everyone's obligations clearly spelled out, since the local partner and local courts may be unfamiliar with Western joint venture conventions. For an emerging market joint venture, the parties should have a buy/sell clause regarding the other's interest within a five-year period. The documentation should strive for precise language. If the business is set up under domestic jurisdiction, disputes over vague wording are likely to be ruled in favor of the local player, who has more political pull than the outsider. In Russia, BP Amoco, the mammoth oil company, received little respect from local courts, which constantly ruled in favor of Russian-owned Tyumen Oil Company, even when its treatment of their Sidanko joint venture was obvious asset stripping.

The exit and legal issues notwithstanding, a joint venture gives the foreign entrant an instant infrastructure of industry knowledge and contracts. In exchange for its established network and local know-how, the domestic player usually wants a "promote" on its equity commitment. The promote can take various forms, but the local's objective is to pay less for its equity on a proportional basis. In numerous instances, I've seen emerging market partners getting the equivalent of a "free" 10 percent equity interest, and then paying in cash or kind for the remaining participation.

Obviously, in any joint venture, the arrangements for board seats, management controls, reporting relationships, and informational requirements should be determined well in advance. Pinning these items down—in unambiguous contractual language—is doubly important in the developing world. The local partner may be unfamiliar with Western expectations on how to handle a business.

GREENFIELD START-UP

Theoretically, a multinational can enter an emerging market on its own, and construct a new operation totally from scratch. This entry arrangement is called a "greenfield" project, since the sites for such start-ups are often virgin lands, or "green fields." The approach has a distinct appeal. Why use a joint venture with a potentially troubling partner? A few multinationals have accomplished this feat, but most prefer to sacrifice some control in order to include a local investor. Greenfield operations are mostly utilized by foreigners in forming manufacturing or service platforms that target the export market. Start-ups are not popular for attacking the local market.

Even a company as powerful and well known as America Online (AOL) enlists a local partner before entering a developing nation. Setting up AOL Latin America in 1998, AOL enlisted Venezuela's Cisneros Group, a prominent conglomerate, to act as AOL's Sherpa in guiding the start-up through the region. The technology, distribution and sales network are designed from the AOL Internet service model, but the local influence is there.

A greenfield project has its advantages. It institutes Western production methods, management techniques, and business cultures right away. It doesn't carry the baggage of the local partner's operations, and it avoids the restructuring problems of the emerging market acquisition. Balanced with the right mix of local investors and managers, it enhances the chances for success in certain industries.

ACQUISITION

Buying an emerging market business can be favorably compared with starting up an entirely new venture, or entering into a halfway arrangement such as a joint venture, passive investment, or marketing alliance. Compared with these alternatives, buying an established enterprise can be a preferable development strategy for four key reasons:

1. *Less risk.* Established businesses that are acquired have a developed customer base, a verifiable financial track record, and a demonstrated product line. The prospective acquisition has long ago passed its most risky phase of corporate life, the start-up.
2. *Infrastructure for growth.* The acquired company's plant, technology, reputation, and employee base provide the buyer with a ready-made infrastructure. Its set of business licenses, operating permits, and import quotas enable the buyer to avoid the bureaucratic maze that accompanies a greenfield. The potential for growth is significantly enhanced if the buyer uses this infrastructure more effectively than the prior owner.
3. *Conservation of capital investment.* As a stand-alone investment, many acquisitions produce income and positive cash flow immediately. Financing corporate growth can be easier via acquisition because lenders and outside investors see the acquisition itself as predictably contributing funds to pay debt service and provide shareholder returns.
4. *Control.* Alternatives to an acquisition—joint ventures, passive equity investments in Third World parties, and marketing/distribu-

tion alliances—require less capital, but offer reduced control. The potential acquirer's return on its investment then depends on someone outside of the corporate umbrella.

On the other hand, while a takeover seems like a low-risk alternative to greenfield expansion, many acquisitions lose money for the buyers. The purchase price may be too high, or the target may have hidden liabilities that cannot be reliably uncovered through due diligence. Cross-cultural problems easily arise between Western executives and emerging market managers that have trouble adapting. That is why a high proportion of multinationals step into emerging markets gradually. They start with exports, then marketing alliances, joint ventures, and small acquisitions. A sizeable deal is a culmination of the long-term entry approach.

A good review of the merger and acquisition process—from considering a strategy to valuing a business and closing the deal—is contained in my first book, *M&A: A Practical Guide to Doing the Deal* (New York: Wiley, 1997).

PRIVATIZATION

Privatization is the transition of an operating business from state ownership to private ownership. The term is the opposite of socialization and was first identified with the sell-off of British state industries under Margaret Thatcher in the 1980s. Since then, privatization has spread to all parts of the globe, including developed and underdeveloped economies.

The rationale is that state-owned enterprises are inherently inefficient and that market discipline is needed to iron out inefficiencies. In the emerging markets, parastatals are generally money-losers, and governments opt to sell these firms to raise money and cut losses.

The 1990s saw a huge volume of privatization in the emerging markets, and developing nations sold every kind of business. The largest deals were associated with oil producers and telephone companies, and tens of billions of dollars were raised. This activity was concentrated in Latin American and Eastern Europe, but Asia and Africa are catching up.

For the most part, the "low hanging fruit" of privatization has been picked. In the earlier deals, the sales process for government businesses was corrupted, and favored groups or individuals bought potentially high-profit business for pennies on the dollar. The principal Russian oligarchs, who now control upwards of 30 percent of the economy, acquired most of their wealth in this manner. Local scandals and multilateral pressures encouraged local governments to retain investment banks, which now conduct auctions of the more valuable properties by approaching a wide range of buyers.

When the government is the seller, versus a family owner, the multinational is likely to see a business that is run down. Common issues include:

- Management and employees view their jobs in a civil service context, rather than a profit-making mode.
- Some employees require under-the-table payments to respond to customer requests.
- Many people on the payroll have political patronage "no-show" jobs. One acquirer of an Argentine privatization couldn't find 3,000 people listed as employees.
- Employees cannot be terminated for any reason, and the business carries multiple social obligations like employee housing and children's' schooling.
- Accounting and cost controls are lax, and the books are unaudited.
- A large portion of accounts receivable are uncollectible. At one telephone company in Africa that I reviewed, receivables equaled two years sales, versus 45 days for the average phone company.
- Recording keeping is poor. Contracts, licenses, permits, agreements, and similar legal documents are often missing.

In exchange for these headaches, the buyer should factor in a high return on investment, and thus a correspondingly lower purchase price. For example, when Holderbank was considering the purchase of government-owned cement firms in Russia, it considered purchase prices of $10 to $15 per ton of annual production capacity. Similar plants in South Korea, Philippines, and India were selling for $40 to $60 per ton.

SUMMARY

An emerging market investment can fatten a multinational's profit margin or increase its growth rate. Offsetting these benefits is the perception of higher risk. Management must assess the tradeoffs before taking the plunge.

Joint ventures, privatizations, and greenfield projects are popular means of entry for the Western corporation. Local participation in any foreign-led transaction is a good idea.

CHAPTER 5

The Export Platform

In Chapter 4, we talked about companies' need to grow, and the corresponding attraction of the emerging markets. In this chapter, we cover the second reason for corporations to enter these nations—the need to be cost-competitive. Companies accomplish this objective by establishing low-cost production platforms that target a Western audience.

Developing nations actively compete for multinationals wishing to set-up export-oriented production facilities, and the governments shower targeted firms with income tax exemptions, tariff reliefs, and other incentives. Home-country insiders are enthusiastic about export platforms. The foreign-owned businesses provide jobs, and they don't compete with oligopolies serving the home market. Furthermore, these same domestic firms sell supplies to the exporters and thus boost their own profits. From the government's standpoint, export platforms generate hard currency, thus supporting the local currency's value and providing cash to pay for imported oil, medicines and other necessities. Multilateral financial institutions, such as the IMF and World Bank, are enthusiastic about developing countries having export bases, and they assist governments in promoting the policies needed to attract the multinational firms.

THE IMPORTANCE OF COST CONTROLS

Besides making money, a corporation's key goal is *survival*. To stay in business, it must accrue sales and profits. The means by which it continues is called the firm's sustained competitive advantage (SCA). Without an SCA, a company's customers are ready for the taking, and its long-term existence is threatened.

Business scholars ascribe sustainable competitive advantages to three basic strategies:

1. *Low costs.* The firm's cost of producing its goods and services is lower than the competition. (Cellose Aracruz' (Brazil) low wood costs give it an advantage over competing pulp firms.)
2. *Differentiation.* The customer perceives that the firm offers something that is unique. (Chanel No. 5 offers a distinct perfume.)
3. *Focus.* The firm selects a narrow customer base that is underserved by the industry. (Wal-Mart started by building stores in small rural towns that Sears and Kmart avoided.)

These advantages occur in various points of a profitable operation, a theme echoed by Michael Porter in his book *Competitive Advantage* (New York: Free Press, 1985):

> *Competitive advantage cannot be understood by looking at a firm as a whole. It stems from the many discrete activities a firm performs in designing, producing, marketing, delivering, and supporting its product. Each of these activities can contribute to a firm's relative cost position and create a basis for differentiation. A cost advantage, for example, may stem from such disparate sources as a low-cost physical distribution system, a highly efficient assembly process, or superior sales force utilization. Differentiation can stem from similarly diverse factors, including the procurement of high quality raw materials, a responsive order entry system, or a superior product design.*

For the owner of an export platform, the emphasis is on reducing costs. He tries to produce a product (or supply a service) in a country where expenses are lower than a comparable First World facility.

VARIABLE COST SAVINGS

In general, the multinational seeks the cheap labor force in the developing country. Wage rates are so low, relative to the First World, that the poor productivity of the domestic workers are easily overcome, either by hiring more of them (relative to a U.S. plant, for example) or running two shifts instead of one. In Shanghai, an assembly line worker in General Motors' factory makes $3.70 an hour. The comparable compensation in the United States is $22.80. In India, labor costs for skilled engineers are one-sixth of those in Europe, according to Ratol Puri, general manager of Moser Baer India, a maker of floppy disks and CDs. Of course, some of the savings are consumed by the extra costs associated with shipping-in parts for assembly, then sending out the finished product and paying tariffs (if any) in the designated Western market.

One problem in applying these cost equations to a new business is that emerging market workers are difficult to lay off or fire. Wages are low, but local unions and governments in many countries are sticklers on requiring firms to maintain a labor force, even in hard times. Potential employers need to keep this fact in mind.

Besides lower labor costs, emerging markets offer a looser regulatory scheme than most developed countries (see Table 5.1).

TABLE 5.1 Variable Cost Benefits to a Multinational Corporation by Using an Emerging Market as an Export Platform

Cost Component	Benefit (+)/ Negative (−)
Labor savings	+
Less regulation	+
Cheaper raw materials	+
Added shipping costs in and out of emerging market	−
Tariffs for importing product to the West	−
Net benefit on variable costs to using export platform	+

Health and safety laws for workers, if they exist, are loosely enforced, and local unions are plaint on such matters. Environmental
regulation and enforcement are far less stringent than in the West,
and government officials are often paid off by polluters to look the
other way, with little fear of criminal penalty. The related savings
on a pulp plant, for example, amount to millions of dollars, and the
relevant construction costs and operating expenses become less
than a similar plant located in a wealthy country like Canada, for
example.

The downside of a multinational seeking loose regulation is the
potential for bad publicity if its emerging market affiliate is exposed.
Exploiting a poor labor force or polluting the environment is
frowned upon in Western society. Penalties might include a consumer
boycott, a lousy public image, and stiffer domestic regulation, all of
which hurt sales, profits, and stock prices. Multinationals hide their
involvement in shady regulatory schemes by holding their investments in anonymous shell companies. Alternatively, they subcontract
production. The local operators follow the multinational's instruc-
tion and bear the brunt of regulatory hassles.

Another attraction in certain emerging markets is the availability
of cheap raw material. The best bargains for a multinational are
found where a natural resource (or its by-product) is a "nontrad-
able" commodity (i.e., a resource that cannot be shipped abroad).
For example, Venezuela has reserves of natural gas that far exceed its
domestic requirements. To date, the government has been unable to
entice a large oil company into investing $1 billion for a gas liquifi-
cation facility, which could ready the country's gas for export. Without an exportable product, the government sells the gas for $0.50 to
$0.60 per Mcf (vs. $3.50 in the United States) to small petrochemical
plants that transform it into methanol and ammonia. These two
products are then loaded onto merchant vessels and shipped abroad.
Mitsubishi of Japan sponsored one such petrochemical plant, called
Jose Methanol.

Similarly, the country's massive Guri hydroelectric dam on the
Orinoco River produces substantial amounts of electricity that aren't

fully used by local industry. Since the excess cannot be efficiently stored, the government offers it to multinationals, under long-term contract, for 60 percent to 80 percent of the going rate in the United States. The low prices attract heavy electricity consumers, such as aluminum producers and iron ore converters. With gas, electricity, and labor cost savings, local projects cut their variable costs by 60 percent, relative to a Canadian or U.S. operation.

In Brazil, a pulp plant spends $70 on the lumber that goes into one ton of pulp. In Alabama, the same plant spends $110 per ton of pulp. With inexpensive labor added to the cheap raw material, operating costs are 30 percent less than in the United States, according to Paul Yeung of the International Finance Corporation.

FIXED COSTS

Depending on the type of facility, the construction cost of a production plant is usually lower in emerging market than in a developed country. The cost of real estate is less, as well as the labor needed to erect the building and install the machinery. In certain cases, the multinational company sacrifices a portion of the savings, since it may need to create infrastructure that is not provided by the local municipality. Common additions include a private electricity generator, a water filtration system, and a highway/rail link. Licenses, operating fees, graft, and local profit participations are standard expenses that mute construction cost savings.

CAPITAL COSTS

Offsetting the benefits of lower variable and construction expenses are the higher capital costs that a Western firm charges to its export platform. The vagaries of political risk compel multinationals to add a minimum of 5 percent to a U.S. rate of return requirement, for example.

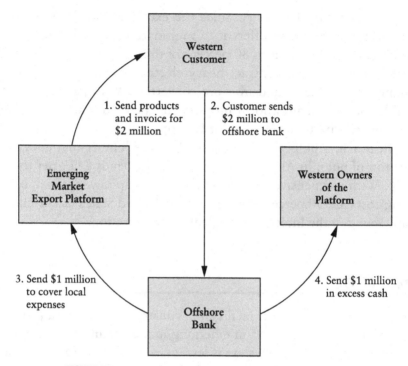

FIGURE 5.1   Export platforms and offshore banks.

Because the export platform sells its products for "hard currency," devaluation in the host country should have little impact on its financial results. To make doubly sure that local governments don't get their hands on that hard currency, the export platform asks its customers to send payments either to its "mother company" or to an offshore bank account. Only enough "hard currency" to run the host country business is then remitted and exchanged into the local money. Emerging market governments frown on this practice, but it is a sound operating procedure for foreign operators (see Figure 5.1):

1. Send products to Western customers.
2. Customers remit payment to export platform's bank account.

3. Export platform directs its bank to send $1 million to host country to cover operating expenses.
4. The remaining $1 million is sent to Western owners and lenders.

Multinationals and Western investors have additional means of extracting hard currency from their export platforms. They can overcharge the platform for imported supplies. On paper, at least, the platform makes less money, pays fewer income taxes, and retains more profits offshore. Another tactic is charging excess management fees to the platform. Instead of billing 1 percent of revenues for a petrochemical plant, the sponsors might ask for 5 percent. Such fees go directly into the hands of the offshore investors, and replace cash dividends that are derived from taxable profits. Alternatively, the foreign sponsor can keep two sets of books, one for its investors, which records the truth, and one for the government, which indicates lessor activity. Third World governments guard against these schemes, but they lack quality enforcement mechanisms.

POPULAR USES OF EXPORT PLATFORMS

Export platforms are most applicable to businesses with the following abilities:

■ *The business manufactures a tangible product, as opposed to a service.* Services are difficult to export. They are time sensitive in nature, require a fair amount of interaction with the customer and frequently have customized components. Advances in telecommunications and Internet capabilities are widening the export of services. Data input and software services are two sectors that India exports to the United States for example. Similarly, General Electric operates call-in centers for global customers in India, and Infosys, an Indian firm with a $12 billion market capitalization, employs 6,000 engineers to export software services. For now, however, tangible products represent the overwhelming balance of trade.

- *The end product's value is represented by a high degree of low-skilled labor content.* Examples include "cut-and-sew" operations for clothing designers and assembly lines for auto part firms.
- *The business is not capital intensive.* The cost of setting-up the platform facility—in terms of new buildings, equipment installation, and related infrastructure—should not be high relative to the value of the product made or assembled. Otherwise, the Western sponsor is subject to the risk of substantial loss if political and currency problems arise.
- *Those semifinished goods and raw materials that are not available locally can be shipped-in with few tariff penalties.* The lifting of tariff barriers for export platforms is the basis for the explosion in the number of *maquiladoras*—export-assembly plants set up along the U.S.–Mexico border by Western multinationals. Foreign-made parts are imported into Mexico, where they are assembled into a finished product and then re-exported.
- *Turnaround time is not a critical element of the product's value.* Some manufacturers need to change their product lines quickly, as customer demands shift. The emerging markets are not for them. The logistics of changing a production process in an emerging market and shipping the finished goods over thousands of miles are complicated, and cannot be accomplished overnight.

Export platforms don't work for certain large industries that operate in the West. A partial list of relevant sectors is set forth in Table 5.2.

NATURAL RESOURCES

Manufacturing and service companies compete on a variety of considerations. Price, quality, reputation, service, brand name, technology, and other differentiating characteristics of their respective product

TABLE 5.2   Inappropriate Sectors for Export Platforms

Industry	Comments
Advertising	Tends to be local and service-oriented.
Autos	High costs of factories and the need for a skilled labor force discourage Third World sites. GM's assembly plant in Pudong, China cost $1.5 billion, for example.
Banking	Customer confidence, rule of law, and stable currency support banking centers in developed nations, rather than emerging markets.
Cable-Television	Transmission lines are local.
Education	Most advanced learning centers are based in the West. Schools need to be close to the students for the most part.
Electricity	Generation sites must be close to the user to restrict transmission drop-off. It is thus impractical to export electricity over long distances.
Entertainment	Emerging market films, music, and books haven't caught-on in the West.
Homebuilding/Construction/ Real Estate	A local business
Insurance	Affiliated with financial centers in the developed nations.
Healthcare	In general, healthcare services are provided near the patient's residence. Emerging markets are not known for their quality healthcare.
Restaurants	Similar to retailers' situation.
Retailing	Stores must be near the customer, although merchandise can originate overseas. Electronic commerce may allow more offshore retailing.
Telecommunications Services	Some export potential for the emerging markets.

lines enable them to compete and succeed in many ways. Natural resource companies, in contrast, participate in commodity markets where the basic product—oil, timber, or iron ore, for example—is essentially the same. The success of these firms is dependent on the regular replacement of resource reserves. As resources in the developed

countries become depleted or subject to stringent environmental regulations, multinational firms look outside their host countries.
Emerging markets are fertile ground.

Nigeria, Venezuela, and Mexico are major oil producers. Brazil is
an important source of iron ore. South Africa sells vast amounts of
diamonds and precious metals. Chile is a major center for copper
mining. This list of natural resource suppliers is supplemented every
year, as more developing nations open their borders to global resource companies.

Natural resources trade globally and they are easily sold for hard
currency. The relevant mining, extraction, and harvesting operations
are therefore suitable export platforms.

Natural resource projects are capital intensive, and huge
amounts are expended for infrastructure and machinery. Labor cost
becomes a secondary item. For example, a respectable gold mine
costs a minimum of $150 million to establish. The going rate for a
300,000 ton-per-year pulp mill is $400 million. These investments
break-the-bank at smaller companies, so natural resource projects in
the emerging markets are sponsored by the largest multinationals.
These massive firms diversify political risk among many nations.
Exxon's exploration arm, for example, is active in dozens of emerging markets.

The size and visibility of a natural resource project require the
sponsors to work closely with the local, regional and national government in planning and implementing the investment. This cooperation
should extend into the ownership arena suggests Steve Robinson, law
partner at Cleary Gottlieb, "It's a good idea to obtain a government
partner, so the government's economic interest is aligned with yours.
This should reduce the problems of political risk." In my experience,
project sponsors provide governments with equity participation of 10
percent to 30 percent, often at a discount compared to the private sector price.

Like any protective strategy, having a government partner is not
always successful. In Vietnam, Erly Industries established an export

FIGURE 5.2 Multinationals explore in remote areas for natural resources.

joint venture with Vinafood, a government-owned rice company. As the product price increased, the government reneged on its promise to supply the venture with rice, and sold through its own agents. When Erly protested this and similar unfair actions, the government launched a sham investigation into embezzlement and came up with bogus accusations of tax fraud. The problems drove the joint venture into bankruptcy, and Erly lost its entire investment.

SUMMARY

Emerging markets represent attractive bases from which multinational firms generate exports. For manufacturing and assembly firms, a developing country offers cheap labor that reduces production costs. For natural resource firms, emerging markets offer the possibility of untapped reserves. The appropriate use of offshore banks reduces the currency risk of the multinational's investment.

CHAPTER 6

Reasons for U.S. Firms to Avoid Emerging Markets

There are plenty of reasons for Western businesses to avoid the emerging markets. For starters, the rich, developed markets represent 80 percent of economic activity. Many opportunities are available in the wealthy countries, and getting in—and out—of an investment is easier and more transparent than in a poor country. Western stockholders legitimately ask: Why put up with the hassle of investing money in these areas? Why not just go and sell our goods there?

Well, you might reply "Third World economic growth rates are strong!" In one sense, that's true. The economies of the emerging markets—on a collective basis—have expanded faster than the developed nations over the last 10 years. However, the record has been uneven. During the last 25 years, for example, East Asia's per capita GNP tripled and South Asia's almost doubled, but the performance of Latin America and Eastern Europe was flat. Africa's economy actually went backwards. All of the regions experienced severe dislocations that reversed prior advances, causing their economies to move two steps forward, only to take one step back. The growth story was not a bed of roses.

Even with strong percentage gains in GNP levels, these countries don't have the buying power to consume a lot of Western goods. And, they won't be significant markets any time soon, because they're starting at such a low base relative to the West. Vietnam's per capita GNP, for example, has increased an average of 6 percent for each of the last 10 years. This is an outstanding performance, but its per capita income levels are only one-tenth of Mexico and one hundredth of the United States. The average Vietnamese won't be able to afford a car for decades.

The economic success that does accrue to the developing economies tends to be concentrated in the hands of a small group. Western consumer companies—used to marketing to a broad middle class—find this niche to be a difficult sell. Meanwhile, the principal customers for business-to-business marketers are the family conglomerates. They know Westerners are anxious to crack their economies, so they don't leave much profit on the table for outsiders. As a result, the growth story supporting investment by multinationals is less than compelling. In fact, it is easier for a Western firm to buy into a prosperous business at home than to canvass the emerging markets for a suitable opportunity. For this reason, a Bear Stearns & Co. executive told me, "the real companies—like General Motors and Colgate Palmolive—don't expect profits immediately. They're in the emerging markets for the long haul—20 years."

GAINING ACCESS

The problem with a U.S. or European firm importing goods into an emerging market is one of access. A poor country's finance ministry doesn't want hard currency exiting its borders unless there's a good reason. If the Western imports are nonessential items—Marlboro cigarettes or Budweiser beer, for example—the government imposes quotas or tariffs to raise the product's price and limit its demand. Even treaties like China's WTO entry don't open markets quickly. "American companies have to be realistic," says Dong Tao, Asian economist at Credit Suisse First Boston, "Genuine market access in China will take years, probably decades." If the Western import can be assembled or manufactured locally, the government pressures the multinational to place a facility in the country. This last action has double benefit for the country in that: it (1) creates new jobs and

(2) provides hard currency. Discussing trade barriers and the emerging markets, Yukio Shotoku, a Matsushita Electric executive, cautions Western firms, "If you have high expectations (after liberalization) you will be disappointed . . . it's unrealistic to expect barriers to be eliminated overnight."

SLOW PACE COMPARED TO A DEVELOPED COUNTRY

The slow pace of the emerging market entry process is apt to frustrate a hard-charging Western businessman. Dominated by a handful of powerful families, most of these countries are essentially closed economies, and the ruling establishment proceeds in a measured way, without worrying about unexpected competitors. (See

FIGURE 6.1 Hard charging Western executives need to slow down in the emerging markets.

Figure 6.1.) For publicly traded multinationals that get graded quarter-to-quarter, the sense of an urgency found in the United States is important, and they can't afford to lose it by getting bogged down overseas.

The slow pace of change in China caused one U.S. telecommunications firm to shutter its Shanghai office. Describing the business environment there, a high-level executive told me, "the future is a lost cause in China; we prefer to go where we can see progress in five years." Matsushita, which invested $700 million in China, lost money in three of the five years between 1995 and 1999, but it expected improvements in 2000.

NORMAL BUSINESS RISKS

Whatever growth potential exists in a place like China, Russia, or Nigeria is shrouded in a cloak of risks. These risks relate not only to the normal uncertainties of any business, but also to the problems specific to the emerging markets.

Let's consider a few business risks that one considers in a Western setting:

- *Demand*—Is there sufficient demand for the business' product or service offerings?
- *Competition/Pricing*—Will existing/future competitors provide a profitable pricing environment?
- *Marketing/Distribution*—Can you reach the potential consumer in a cost-effective manner?
- *Suppliers*—Can suppliers deliver quality materials, parts and services on a timely basis?
- *Workforce*—Will the workforce perform as expected?
- *Management*—Is experienced management available to run the business?
- *Financing*—Will lenders and equity investors provide financing at a reasonable cost for maintaining and expanding the business?

The challenge of managing these risks and sustaining a profitable business is considerable. Many Western firms fail, get acquired, or go bankrupt.

NORMAL BUSINESS RISKS AND THE EMERGING MARKETS

For an emerging market investment, this list of "normal risks" takes on added meaning. Extra precautions must be taken. For example, in the United States, when you turn on a light switch, the electricity goes on. In Tajikistan, this simple action places you in the realm of probability theory. A substantial percentage of the time, the lights stay dark, thus demonstrating the need for a prospective factory to have an expensive back-up generator.

Basic information sources must be double-checked in these locales. If your marketing plan calls for print advertising, make an extra effort to verify the circulation statistics of local publications. Approach demand forecasts by using multiple references, and compare them to independent studies prepared by Western consulting firms. Beware of consulting firms and "experts" that rely on the same source data.

Once you've made a demand and pricing forecast, contrast it to similar product introductions in countries with comparable economic and cultural characteristics. A Western firm considering a telecom investment in Romania might base its projections on the following hypothesis: Romanians will use their cellular phones about the same as Bulgarians. The firm assumes that the Romanian demand will mirror the Bulgarian experience. This methodology puts the forecaster in the right ballpark, but miscalculations are common. By way of illustration, Western phone companies and investment firms bought stakes in nascent Indian cellular firms, based on the rapid acceptance of the technology elsewhere in Asia. Indian customers started buying the phones, but their monthly usage (in minutes) was way below other Asians. The cellular companies missed their sales projections, and the investors lost millions.

WHY WERE THE CONSTRUCTION CRANES NOT MOVING?

An emerging market venture should have an extra margin of financial safety. Too much reliance on local sources of debt financing causes problems, particularly in the severe downturns that affect these nations on an intermittent basis. Banks refuse to lend money, and a well-documented credit line—with all of its legality—may not help. After the Korean won crashed in 1997, the government encouraged local banks to stop credit expansion, and they followed this directive religiously. The economic dislocation from this sudden cutoff soon required another government edict, which encouraged the banks to open working capital lines for the country's biggest employers, like Hyundai and Daewoo. Left out of the loop were real estate developers, who require regular borrowings. They were especially hard hit when credit dried up. Visiting Seoul in 1998, I saw dozens of their construction cranes at a complete standstill. The lesson for the foreign-owned operation is to obtain insurance by signing back-up credit agreements with foreign banks. The related documentation should have minimal "exits" for the lenders, who'll want to bail out if local conditions deteriorate.

SPECIFIC RISKS FOR THE EMERGING MARKETS

Besides the risks attendant to any business venture, emerging market opportunities involve a set of issues that don't figure prominently in the United States, Western Europe, or Japan. These concerns fall into four broad categories:

1. Political risk.
2. Macroeconomic risk.
3. Currency risk.
4. Information risk.

The extra risks curtail the benefits of higher growth, and limit the margin of error for the investor (see Figure 6.2). This conundrum led one fund manager to confide in me, "Emerging market equities can never beat the S&P 500 over the long term—everything has to go right with these companies! Not only must the businesses operate as planned, but the political and currency environments have to cooperate. The positive confluence of these items never happens on a sustained basis." Recent years have been difficult for foreign businesses. Merchant International Group surveyed 7,500 multinationals and found that 84 percent of their operations spawned in the emerging markets in the late 1990s failed to meet financial targets.

Political Risk

The term *political risk* covers a broad range of uncertainties that affect the value of an investment. The best known of these risks is expropriation, whereby a local government takes over a foreign-owned

FIGURE 6.2 Western businesspeople need to fight off the four key risks.

operation and offers little or no recompense to the stockholders. In 1979, Brazil expropriated Light S.A.—the mammoth Rio de Janeiro electric company—which had been founded by Canadian investors. This action attracted much publicity, but the incidence of outright expropriation over the last 20 years has virtually ceased. Developing nations now embrace capitalistic policies and realize that outright confiscation portrays the government in a bad light. A better tactic is to implement a "creeping expropriation," whereby the foreign-owned business is subject to death by a thousand cuts. Small, continuous, and onerous changes in regulatory, tax, and currency policies grind down Western owners. These official actions are then combined with serial misdeeds by local partners, such as violating contractual understandings or padding the shareholder ledger to dilute foreigners' control. Eventually, such problems convince the outsiders to sell at a bargain price.

Rapid Changes in Government Policies.   When Western nations alter policies toward foreign investment, the changes are generally gradual and incremental in nature. The state of development of Third World political systems, however, makes them susceptible to dramatic changes stemming from economic hardship, failed government efforts, and social or ethnic instability. Popular dissatisfaction with a status quo may lead to revisions or rejections of laws and policies favoring multinational investment.

In the late 1990s, for example, Indonesia, which had been a model of stability, underwent a sea change in its business environment. President Suharto left office with no successor, the currency collapsed, a deep recession set in, Indonesians ransacked Chinese businesses, the East Timor civil war flared up, a banking crisis got worse, and students protested corruption. The clubby relationships between the multinationals and their Suharto cronies fractured as aid agencies and local reformers examined business practices within the country. As one example, Asia Pulp & Paper, a major conglomerate earned huge profits from a sweetheart lumber concession on the island of Sumatra, and analysts speculated whether the arrangement would hold-up under scrutiny.

Civil War and Insurrection. At times, the political instability of an emerging market spills over into armed conflict. Offices and factories—both domestic and foreign-owned—are damaged or destroyed. During the break-up of Yugoslavia, foreign lenders lost millions as their collateral was reduced to rubble by civil war.

No matter how much financial and political analysis an investor does, predicting violent conflict is difficult. Noted value investor, Jean Marie Eveillard, likes to base decisions on careful evaluations of individual companies, but he acknowledges, "I lay awake at night worrying that North Korea might invade South Korea."

When governments are toppled by revolutions, the new leaders sometimes insist that the old regime's obligations don't apply to the new order. After the Muslim fundamentalists removed the Shah of Iran, they initially refused to pay the country's debts to international corporations and banks. Although they later backed off this extreme position, their liability situation is not fully resolved 25 years later.

Rule of Law/Legal Discrimination. In general, emerging markets lack fully developed legal systems and the bodies of commercial law and practice normally found in the Western nations. Laws affecting international investment and business continue to evolve, although at times in an uncertain and arbitrary manner that may not coincide with accepted international practices. Inconsistencies and discrepancies among the vast number of local, regional, and national laws, the lack of judicial and legislative guidance on unclear laws, and the broad discretion on the part of authorities implementing the laws produce additional uncertainties. The overall impact of this situation is to make foreign investors wary. Commenting on the Russian television environment, Raymond Joslin, president of Hearst Entertainment & Syndication, provides a typical reaction, "There will be no serious investment until there is a system of jurisprudence."

The dispute resolution process in an emerging market court system is extremely slow, and final judicial decisions on commercial matters can easily take 5 to 10 years before appeals are exhausted. Even then, the ability of a plaintiff to enforce a favorable judgment may pose additional problems of a lengthy duration.

The situation was illustrated during the recent financial crises. Few lenders forced their delinquent emerging market borrowers into bankruptcy. They correctly reasoned that accelerating debts in this manner made little sense, since it would have placed the borrower under a court's supervision. With a judicial overseer, the reorganization or liquidation of a substantial business requires a minimum of six years and more likely 10 years. The end results are uncertain, because the judge has little case law to guide him. For this reason, foreign lenders avoid placing borrowers into bankruptcy. Lenders negotiate with distressed clients for several years to reach a settlement, and they generally allow the borrower some breathing room by suspending interest and principal payments. By way of illustration, the 1980s debt restructuring of Fomento Mexicana de Desaroll, the Mexican conglomerate, took six years.

The local business communities have lived with convoluted legal systems for years, and local companies are the victims of capricious court rulings as well as foreigners. "The likelihood of discrimination increases the more a firm is perceived as an outsider within the legal jurisdiction," says Javier Echeverrey, an Argentine lawyer. Thus, a Buenos Aires company might experience problems fighting a lawsuit in Neuguen, which is 900 hundred miles from the Argentine capital. In the provinces, the local jurists and business owners know each other well, and the chances of illegal cooperation increases. For Western firms operating in the Third World, the "outsider notion" is more pronounced, particularly as the legal jurisdiction moves outward from the large cities, where most international business is conducted.

A dispute against one of the large, family-controlled conglomerates may hinge on relative strengths. A small company—either local or foreign—is at a disadvantage for two reasons: (1) it may not have the ability to finance a protracted legal battle against a deep-pocketed adversary; or (2) it may not want to take on an enterprise that has substantial purchasing power and economic influence. In contrast, a big firm/big firm dispute presents no inherent advantages for either side. In fact, a lawsuit involving a prominent Western plaintiff, like Sony, may actually weaken the local's chances, as such a case draws international scrutiny.

In negotiating a sizeable contract with a local operator, the foreign investor should request that the contract be governed by a developed jurisdiction, such as the United States or United Kingdom. The contract should have a mandatory arbitration clause for disputes, with arbitration conducted by an officially-sanctioned body in a neutral location. If the foreigner settles for local jurisdiction, the contract should be governed by a national court or a "big city" court where the judges are familiar with international business. As noted, in the outlying provinces of these countries, Westerners have problems.

"Winning" an arbitration doesn't mean collecting money, however. In 1985, the Electric Company of Ecuador (under U.S. investor ownership) won a $52 million ruling from an arbitration panel, which concluded that the Ecuadorian government had broken its contract. Sixteen years later, the judgment remains uncollected and this company, after exhausting its legal means of redress, has taken to hiring high-priced Washington lobbyists to get a hearing at the U.S. State Department.

Contacting your local embassy is one tactic for seeking relief from unfair treatment. Unless your employer is a large visible firm in its home country—like Goldman Sachs Group in the United States—don't expect your consular officials to run much interference. They're understaffed and have more pressing concerns than small commercial disputes.

Political risk insurance policies offer some protection against legal discrimination. The problem for the insured is collecting on a claim. The insurance company wants the multinational to first run the lengthy legal gauntlet. Should its client lose the case, and demand payment, the insurance company can contest the assertion of discrimination, imposing a further delay.

Crime and Corruption.   Official corruption and organized crime are common in developing countries, and more overt than in the West. The resultant bribes and payoffs—done directly or through intermediaries such as consultants, agents, or advisors—increase the cost of doing business for local companies as well as foreign investors. As outsiders that are perceived to be wealthier than the locals, Western companies are logical targets for these shenanigans.

For example, when I worked on a project financing in Venezuela, professional engineers from the United States and England reviewed construction cost estimates for the foreign bank syndicate. On a confidential basis, they informed me that local contractors, engineers, and architects routinely padded bills by 15 percent to 30 percent. The surplus covered black market payments required to move the project along. "Transaction costs are 25 percent to 30 percent of a deal in Central Asia. Getting this changed will take a very long time," says Hudson Thornber a Moscow-based consultant for Arthur Andersen. Even the European Bank for Reconstruction and Development, a cheerleader for these markets, admits that the average cost of bribery is 6 percent of company revenue in Russia and as much as 8 percent in Georgia.

Another example is related by Control Risks Groups. A Western company considered buying a factory in Kazakhstan. It was an attractive opportunity, but a preinvestment audit revealed that product and raw materials worth $2 million had disappeared in the previous 12 months. An investigation led by Control Risks revealed the real situation. Actual levels of theft were $15 million per year (rather than $2 million). Organized crime had infiltrated the factory and was diverting products. The management team was corrupt and the staff so badly and irregularly paid that they were forced to steal to survive. The local police and judiciary were paid to turn a blind eye.

New management is sometimes the answer, explains Jack Perkowski, executive at Asimco, which has acquired several Asian firms. "If the head of your purchasing department has lived his whole life in the city where the plant is located, there's going to be trouble," Perkowski argues. "He's going to have all sorts of relationships—friends, family members. You have to break those ties to have a profitable company."

Certain countries have gangs that target employees of multinationals as potential victims of theft, kidnapping, and extortion. Local police departments are generally ineffective in stopping the criminal element. In Columbia, for example, the rate of murders to court convictions is approximately 100 to 1. In certain countries, the evidence shows that police frequently cooperate with the criminals. Many large businesses in the Third World employ private security forces as a result. Although I never had a personal security problem in my travels, the issue was personally brought home at a fancy cocktail party held in an exclusive suburb of Cali, Columbia. Attended by the cream of Cali's society, the event featured a musical group imported from Miami to entertain the guests with American show tunes. Tuxedoed waiters served the guests with choice hors d'oeuvres until 11 P.M. when a delicious dinner was served accompanied by fine wines from Europe and California. Lurking in the driveway and lawns of the beautiful estate—and not too far way from the festivities—were the attendees' numerous bodyguards, all armed with pistols, shotguns, and Uzi machine guns. The differences between the goings-on inside—and the security outside—was both stark and illuminating.

Grey Market/Nonenforcement Issues. The close ties between government and local businesses result—and could in the future result—in preferential treatment, arbitrary decisions, and other practices that adversely affect foreign investment. Some of these practices are clearly illegal, while others fall into a grey area. As noted earlier, elite family dominance, tradition, xenophobia, and closed-market syndrome contribute to this environment. Newcomers must be careful about their entry tactics.

In certain situations, a Western firm's progress can be slowed through inaction by governments, unions, and potential suppliers. In China, factories making counterfeit designer clothes operate openly.

They close temporarily when firms like Louis Vuitton and Channel embarrass the local authorities into shutting down the transgressors. U.S. cement companies cannot import cement into Mexico. Custom inspectors halt the U.S. product at the border for bogus "inspections," local transport unions refuse to handle U.S. cement, and Mexican distributors avoid selling it to please the resident oligopoly. Global retail chains like Wal-Mart and Toys 'R' Us have problems cutting through similar "nontariff" barriers. Third World officials drag their feet on zoning issues and old-line developers refuse to sell them land for fear of alienating established retailers.

In forming its semiconductor joint venture in China, Taiwan's Hung Jen group sought to avoid such risks. As its partner, it selected Jiang Mianheng, son of China's President Jiang Zemin.

Measuring Political Risk.   Most Western investors with whom I've worked consider a country's political risk by combining a number of factors: personal experience, friends' and colleagues' experience, a country's history, published news sources, and risk analysis services. The measurement process is highly qualitative, and the degree of uncertainty varies, depending on the country, industry, partner, and transaction in question.

If a multinational concludes that it can do business without being cheated, the next issue is: Can we successfully exit the investment in the future? Assuming the answer is "yes," a minimum rate-of-return threshold is established, taking into account the relative risk assumed. Higher risk countries should generate higher returns. My experience indicates that foreign investors have the following IRR targets for low-tech manufacturing and service businesses: low-risk countries (e.g., Mexico), 15 percent to 20 percent; medium-risk countries (e.g., India), 20 percent to 30 percent; and high-risk countries (e.g., Gambia), 30 percent to 40 percent.

A number of companies provide political risk analysis services that quantify—in one number or one word—the relative risk that an outsider takes on in a given country. A list of providers appears as follows:

■ Bank of America World Information Service.
■ Business Environment Risk Intelligence, S.A.
■ Control Risks Information Services.
■ Economist Intelligence Unit.
■ Euromoney Institutional Investor.
■ Merchant International Group.
■ Political Risk Services: ICRG.
■ Political Risk Service—Coplin—O'Leary Rating.

Hedging against Political Risk. The best protection a Westerner has against political risk is a strong and reputable local partner, who can run interference against local elements that want to harm the foreign investment. In most countries, the candidates meeting this definition of "partner" are either a large family conglomerate or the national government.

Of course, the strategy doesn't always work. Through privatization, Southern Company and AES gained control (for $1 billion) of Brazilian power company, Energia de Minar Gerais. The provincial government, which was a partner in the deal, broke its own agreement to give the U.S. firms operating control.

For small Western firms, bringing in a large multinational as a co-investor is a good tactic (see Table 6.1). The big partner can make noise with the foreign embassies and local media when there's a problem. A small firm, however, is just ignored.

TABLE 6.1 How Can a Western Company Limit Its Political Risk in an Emerging Market?

1. Enlist a prominent local company to participate in the venture.
2. Invite the country's federal government to own a portion of the business.
3. Ask a large Western company to invest in the business.
4. Buy political risk insurance from insurance companies, Western governments or multinational banks.
5. Borrow money from First World export-import (ExIm) banks.
6. Have multinational banks lend money to the venture, or invest in the equity.

Another good idea is to have the multilaterals and export-import banks participate in the venture's financing. The export-import banks carry "big sticks" as agencies of their respective governments, should a political action endanger a borrower. The World Bank and its sister organizations conduct active private lending and investment programs. Having such a partner—even if their participation is small—is worthwhile insurance, particularly in the lesser nations, because the governments are reluctant to offend the multilaterals. Besides extending billions of dollars in development loans to these countries, the development banks are influential in providing them with a "Good Housekeeping Seal of Approval." This approval is a perequisite for Western bankers to extend credit. However, keep in mind one fact. These organizations are hard to do business with. I worked in the World Bank's private sector affiliate for five years, and saw the commercial borrowers' frustrations.

The Jose Methanol project in Venezuela used a "belt and suspenders" approach to minimizing political risk. It incorporated a Japanese sponsor (Mitsubishi), a local corporate partner, the Venezuelan government, a World Bank investment, and a U.S. Export-Import Bank guarantee. A Mitsubishi executive told me, "we built an artificial economy in Venezuela, thanks to the World Bank and the U.S. government."

Macroeconomic Risk

Developed economies generally experience smooth growth patterns, interrupted by periodic recessions. After five to six years of 1 percent to 3 percent annual growth, a mild recession of negative 0.5 percent to 1.5 percent growth sets in perhaps for six to twelve months. In contrast, emerging markets are known for repeated boom-and-bust cycles, caused largely by wrongheaded government policies and collapses of investor confidence. A four- or five-year period of 5 percent to 6 percent annual growth is interrupted by severe downturns, when economic activity declines by 7 percent to 8 percent for periods of two years or longer. The cyclical pattern is summarized well by Arminio Fraga, president of Brazil's Central Bank, "It was if we'd (Brazil) get drunk, have a good time, and then after that would come a terrible hangover."

The downturns can be painful for investors, as GDP swings are magnified by value indices, such as the stock market. Russia's default in 1998 caused its stock market to decline by 84 percent. George Soros (the legendary hedge fund manager) and his partners, put $1.8 billion into Russian phone company, OAO Svyazinvest, at the top of the market. Watching the shares' value collapse, he later called it the worst investment he'd ever made. Of course, volatility is two-sided. Since its bottom, the Russian stock index has climbed over 400 percent, making early bottom-fishers look like geniuses.

Vietnam was attractive in the mid-1990s and American firms piled-in, investing over $1 billion. Ford Motor built a $102 million joint venture factory with the capacity to make 14,000 cars a year. In 1999, it sold 400. Procter & Gamble and Pepsi continue to lose money there.

The economic volatility plays havoc with the prediction of demand and pricing. Most corporate investments in the emerging market are predicated on a stable upward move in GNP, which then provides a stable environment for product launches. The typical projection appears in Table 6.2.

Table 6.2 shows a smooth upward curvature. A realistic projection, however, includes a "stress test" every four or five years, to determine if the investment's IRR can survive the regular, but

TABLE 6.2 Typical Western Company Projection of an Emerging Market Venture

	2001	2002	2003	2004	2005
GNP growth	4.0%	4.0%	4.5%	4.5%	5.0%
Product price (US$)	$1.50	$1.58	$1.65	$1.75	$1.86
Divisional sales (millions)	$32.0	$34.0	$37.0	$40.0	$44.0

TABLE 6.3   Realistic Projection of an Emerging Market Venture

	2001	2002	2003	2004	2005
GNP growth	4.0%	4.0%	4.5%	−4.0%	−1.0%
Product price (US$)	$1.50	$1.58	$1.65	$1.43	$1.56
Divisional sales (millions)	$32.0	$34.0	$37.0	$30.0	$32.0
	Prosperity			Recession	

unexpected, shocks. In Table 6.3, we assume a deep recession in the year 2004, and the impact on pricing and sales becomes considerable.

Thus, a practical way of hedging against macroeconomic risk is to make sure your project achieves a reasonable rate of return under pessimistic economic scenarios (see Figure 6.3), as well as steady-state forecasts.

Currency Risk

Most emerging markets attempt to manage their foreign exchange rates, so the value of a currency is not tied strictly to the laws of supply

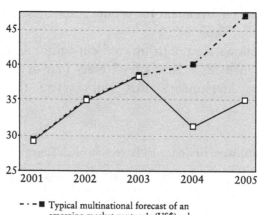

- – · – ■ Typical multinational forecast of an
         emerging market venture's (US$) sales

———□ Realistic forecast

FIGURE 6.3   Naive forecasts vs. reality.

and demand. The typical central bank allows its currency's value to fluctuate within a narrow band of value that is "pegged" to a preeminent First World currency, like the U.S. dollar. If the value of the local currency falls below the band, the bank buys the currency, increasing its value. Should it move above the band, the bank sells, and the value drops.

Deficit spending and a loose monetary policy suggest that a developing country's currency depreciates faster than the U.S. dollar. Responsible central banks signal foreign exchange traders, regarding the speed at which the peg will "slip" against the dollar. Until recently for example, the Turkish band slipped by a fraction of a cent each day.

From time to time, this orderly framework crumbles, as selling pressure builds on a currency. The Central Bank runs out of the foreign-exchange it uses to support the local currency, and it abruptly abandons the peg, allowing the currency to find a new level. The multilaterals and the G-7 nations rush-in to work with the affected country, not only to restore confidence in the currency, but to prevent a domino effect of investors fleeing other markets. After order is restored, the Central Bank establishes a new trading range for the currency. This process is called a *devaluation,* and it involves the local currency declining in value (vis-à-vis the U.S. dollar) by a sizeable amount, perhaps 20 percent to 50 percent in a single month (see Figure 6.4).

Hedging Currency Risk. In a U.S., Japanese, or Western European setting, investors hedge their foreign exchange exposure by utilizing long-dated futures contracts. Unfortunately, the emerging markets lack these contracts, so multinationals use alternative tactics.

The simplest device for avoiding the risk is to focus on export platforms or natural resource projects. Revenues are denominated in U.S. dollars and sent to an offshore bank. Certain raw material costs are indexed to the dollar. Local content and labor expense drop in U.S. dollar terms during a devaluation, thus enhancing a project's profitability. Such investments are well insulated from the local currency regime.

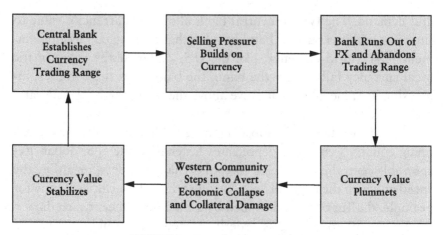

FIGURE 6.4   Devaluation process.

Foreign companies that manufacture for the local market may want to configure their operations for possible exports. APASCO, the Mexican cement maker owned by Swiss-based Holderbank, situated two of its plants near ocean ports. APASCO equipped the ports with costly loading terminals, even though Mexico was importing cement at the time. When a major devaluation hit the country in 1995, cement demand dried up, and APASCO picked-up the slack by shipping their product to Japan, South America, and California. The impact of the currency problem was thereby reduced.

Another way to limit currency risk is to finance a portion of the business with local institutions. Short-term loans and leases are denominated in the domestic currency. When a devaluation occurs, the business suffers fewer financial penalties. Tables 6.4 through 6.7 provides a comparison of using foreign versus domestic debt. Note how the use of domestic debt reduces losses during a devaluation.

Tables 6.4 to 6.7 indicate the inherent dangers for local firms borrowing in U.S. dollars. Nevertheless, many of the Third World companies that I worked with had substantial U.S. dollar debts. The effective interest cost of their U.S. dollar borrowings—translated into local currency equivalents—was lower than domestic loans. For

TABLE 6.4 Joint Venture Results before a Devaluation

Balance Sheet Items at December 31, 2001 (in Millions)

	Scenario 1 100% U.S. Dollar Debt		Scenario 2 100% Domestic Currency Debt		Scenarios 1 and 2 U.S. Dollar Equivalent
Assets	Ps. 100.0	Assets	Ps. 100.0		$50.00
Current liabilities	Ps. 20.0	Current Liabilities	Ps. 20.0		$10.00
Debt (US$25MM)	50.0	Debt (Domestic)	50.0		25.00
Equity	30.0	Equity	30.0		15.00
	Ps. 100.0		Ps. 100.0		$50.00

Note: Balance sheets are numerically the same under both scenarios. Income statements are identical, as set forth in Table 6.5.

example, a sizeable Columbian manufacturer paid 10 percent per year for U.S. dollar loans from J.P. Morgan, when Columbian lenders charged 25 percent or more. For corporate borrowers, the 15 percent annual savings was significant, and they balanced this benefit against a devaluation risk. If the local currency devalued 75 percent or less (against the US$) every five years, the decision was a wash.

TABLE 6.5 Income Statement Items

For the Year Ended December 31, 2001 (in Millions)

	Scenarios 1 and 2	
Revenues	Ps. 90.0	US$ 45.0
EBIT	13.0	$6.5
Interest	5.0	2.5
Pretax income	8.0	4.0
Income taxes	2.0	1.0
Net income	Ps. 6.0	US$ 3.0

Note: Exchange rate is 2 Pesos (Ps.) equals US$ 1.00.

TABLE 6.6 Joint Venture Results after a Devaluation. The Exchange Rate Drops from 2 Ps./US$ 1.00 to 4 Ps./US$ 1.00

	Balance Sheet Items at December 31, 2001			
	Scenario 1 100% U.S. Dollar Debt		Scenario 2 100% Domestic Currency Debt	
	Ps.	US$	Ps.	US$
Assets	Ps. 100.0	$25.0	Ps. 100.0	$25.0
Current liabilities	Ps. 20.0	$ 5.0	Ps. 20.0	$ 5.0
Debt	100.0	25.0	50.0	12.5
Equity	(20.0)	(5.0)	30.0	7.5
	Ps. 100.0	$25.0	Ps. 100.0	$25.0

Notes: Under Scenario 1, the write-up of the US$ debt after the devaluation causes shareholders' equity to sink into negative numbers.
Under Scenario 2, shareholder value drops to US$ 7.5 million equivalent (from the predevaluation number of $15.0 million) but it is far above Scenario 1's negative result.

Borrowers look to outside consultants that assess devaluation probabilities. Several services that provide political risk analysis also evaluate currency risk. The bond ratings of the principal credit agencies are a proxy for currency risk. And finally, numerous Wall Street firms and commercial banks report on the likelihood of devaluations.

Information Risk

In evaluating existing businesses in the emerging markets, Western firms should remember that the quality of information is not on par with the United States. Furthermore, the information that is provided may not be available in English, prompting heavy translation costs. This situation calls for an extra level of due diligence, and an acknowledgement that decisions must be made with information that is 50 percent to 75 percent of the amount expected in a developed country deal.

TABLE 6.7 Joint Venture Results after Devaluation. The Exchange Rate Drops from 2 Ps./US$ 1.00 to 4 Ps./US$ 1.00

		Income Statement Data			
		After			
		Scenario 1 100% U.S. Dollar Debt		Scenario 2 100% Domestic Currency Debt	
	Before	Ps.	US$	Ps.	US$
Revenues	Ps. 90.0	Ps. 90.0	$22.5	Ps. 90.0	$22.5
EBIT	Ps. 13.0	Ps. 13.0	$ 3.3	Ps. 13.0	$ 3.3
Interest	5.0	10.0	2.5	5.0	1.3
Pretax income	8.0	3.0	0.8	8.0	2.0
Income taxes	2.0	0.8	0.2	2.0	0.5
Net income	Ps. 6.0	Ps. 2.2	$ 0.6	Ps. 6.0	$ 1.5

Notes: Under Scenario 1, net income (in local currency terms) drops from Ps. 6.0 million to Ps. 2.2 million. Interest cost (derived from US$ debt) jumps from Ps. 5.0 million to Ps. 10.0 million.

Under Scenario 2, net income (in local currency) is stable at Ps. 6.0 million. The devaluation decreases US$ equivalent net income to $1.5 million from $3.0 million.

Company-Specific Information Risk. At the company-specific level, emerging market firms do not generate the kind of management information that Western firms produce. Details on production cost data, customer histories, and supplier arrangements may be scanty or nonexistent. Management information systems may be underdeveloped, and business planning may be informal and subject to the Chairman's whims. In one of my South Korean transactions, important real estate titles, factory operating permits and equipment leases were missing from the company's files.

Emerging market accounting firms—including the branches of the Big Five—are more compliant in bending toward management's wishes than their Western counterparts, so foreigners should ask a lot of questions that are considered elementary in a U.S. or European setting.

For example, in 1998 I discussed the financial statements of a Thai satellite broadcasting company with its chief financial officer. Consider the following items that covered tens of millions of dollars:

- *Accounts receivable.* The auditors did not increase the loss reserve on accounts receivable, despite the fact that the economic crisis had placed many of the firm's customers into insolvency.
- *Real estate.* Real estate values had plunged 80 percent in downtown Bangkok, but the auditors didn't write down the value of the headquarters building.
- *Long-term contract.* The counterparty to a long-term contract was in a distressed condition. It was unlikely to fulfill its side of the deal, but this fact was missing from the financial statements.
- *Investments.* With its excess cash, the company had made sizeable investments in the Bangkok stock market, as well as equity investments in several unlisted firms. The auditors had not marked these items to market, despite the dramatic decline in the Bangkok stock index.
- *Anticipated long-term financing.* An American satellite manufacturer had promised to provide substantial financing for a new satellite. Given the crisis, the cancellation of this arrangement was probable, yet the accountants failed to mention this possibility, even though it threatened the business as a "going concern."

The auditors protected the broadcaster from revealing its dire financial condition to outsiders, and the management group left it up to foreigners to ask the right questions.

Local accounting conventions can diverge significantly from U.S. Generally Accepted Accounting Principles (GAAP). A reasonable understanding of the differences is easy to achieve, and you can covert a local firm's numbers into U.S. conventions quickly. Obtaining the information to achieve this conversion, however, is no cakewalk. Management and its constituents are reluctant to release details on sweetheart contracts, insider deals, and undisclosed contingent liabilities. These concerns are particularly acute in countries like South Korea, where (a) large companies are closely involved with a web of interlocking firms (i.e., a *cheobol*), (b) financial statements are not consolidated (this is changing), and (c) contingent liabilities are not disclosed in financial reports.

South Korean investment bankers joke that publicly traded Korean firms have three sets of books: one for stock exchange filings, one for the tax authorities, and one for the family. In one of my Korean deals, sorting out the true economic results was problematic. The management didn't quite understand my employer's need for due diligence, and they were reluctant (or unable) to supply documented evidence of representations. Their Korean audit firm was uncooperative, and claimed client privilege in refusing to talk with Westerners. The company's lead bank refused an interview and accepted written questions only. The bank's answers contradicted the company's views on the debt guarantees of its fellow *cheobol* members.

We enlisted the Seoul office of Price Waterhouse, at a $50,000 fee, to conduct a "businessman's due diligence" on our behalf. The accounting firm sent a long report three weeks later, but it was suprisingly superficial. Price Waterhouse did no sampling or independent checking of the Korean company's assertions. Buried deep in the text was the fact that Price Waterhouse relied totally on the representations of the other auditor and the company's management. When I complained and questioned why they didn't review the other auditor's work papers, Price Waterhouse replied that "this wasn't done in Korea" and that "local auditors don't let anyone review their work product." Lesson learned: Make sure your advisors' due diligence process corresponds to Western standards.

In the end, my employer went ahead with the deal, a $32 million investment with Shinmoorim Paper. By the time Price Waterhouse's report was released, the legal documentation was almost complete, and no one wanted to derail the transaction on what the Koreans considered an accounting technicality. Luckily, we bought convertible bonds. If the company's books had been cooked and problems had arisen, the debt's senior position would have given us an advantage over the common stockholders.

Stuart Poole-Robb, Chief Executive Officer of Merchant International Group, an English consulting firm, is a strong advocate of intense due diligence, "Too often, western firms ignore realities in the emerging markets. Decisions are made by top-level executives who fly in for a day, stay at a downtown hotel, visit the plant, and fly out the next morning. That's no way to evaluate a project properly."

Industry and Macroeconomic Information Risk. Emerging market investors have to be prepared to make decisions on less economic information than is available in the developed nations. Statistics on a given industry may be scanty or non existent. Macroeconomic data prepared by the government or outside groups may be out-of-date, incomplete or erroneous.

To illustrate, in 1998 the Director of the Russian State Committee on Statistics and a number of his subordinates were arrested and charged with manipulating economic data to hide the actual output of various companies, thereby reducing the tax liability of these companies. In 2000, Pakistan agreed to repay $55 million in IMF loans that it obtained when it understated its budget deficits to qualify for IMF support. Tom Rawski, an economic professor at the University of Pittsburgh, suggested China's official GDP growth numbers for 1997 and 1998 were overstated by several percentage points. Observers attributed the exaggeration to state statisticians submitting to political pressure.

The international community is well aware of the information deficiencies. An independent task force sponsored by the Council of Foreign Relations studied the 1994/1995 Mexican crisis and concluded that full financial information was not forthcoming to all investors. The IMF agreed with this conclusion in separate studies. To improve the efficiency of markets, it established the Special Data Dissemination and Standards Program to encourage nations to provide timely and accurate economic statistics. Unfortunately, this program, like many IMF initiatives, was overtaken by events. A short two years later, the Asian crisis hit, caused in part, by the poor quality of economic data made available to investors.

As a Principal Investment Officer of the World Bank Group, I was surprised at how the Bank lent hundreds of millions to developing nations that functioned with unaudited financial statements and minimal

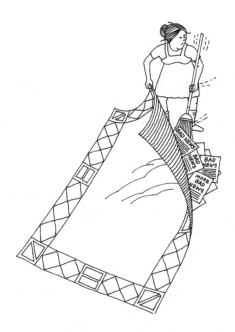

FIGURE 6.5 Sometimes, emerging market authorities sweep bad economic news under the rug.

bookkeeping standards (see Figure 6.5). Similarly, Moody's and Standard & Poor's, the premier credit rating agencies, take most sovereign statistics at face value, and, as a result, they were seriously behind the curve before the 1997 Asian collapse. Government officials at developing countries decry audited financial statements as an infringement on their national sovereignty, but it's obvious that a high degree of transparency facilitates economic development in the long run.

Limiting Information Risk. How to avoid the problems created by information deficiencies? "Potential investors are well advised to use a multidisciplinary team to gather information and assess the business risk," suggests David Bittner, manager at Control Risks Group. A team can comprise:

■ Business executives.
■ Lawyers.

- Forensic accountants.
- Bankers.
- Diplomats.
- Former law enforcement and intelligence officers.
- Information technology specialists.
- Engineering, environmental, and human resources consultants.
- Journalists.
- Political risk consultants.

This range of experience ensures that all the bases are covered, thus reducing the unpredictable nature of investing in a Third World enterprise (see Table 6.8).

TABLE 6.8 How Does a Western Company Limit Emerging Market Risks?

Political Risk	■ Bring in a strong local corporate partner ■ Enlist the government as a partner ■ Recruit a major Western multinational as a partner ■ Utilize investment funds (or guarantees) from the World Bank, other multilaterals, or ExIm banks ■ Buy political risk insurance ■ Insist on detailed legal documentation ■ Provide for legal jurisdiction in New York or London
Economic Risk	■ Use conservative projections ■ Assume one severe recession/devaluation every five years in the projections ■ Have flexibility to export during a downturn
Currency Risk	■ Invest in an export platform ■ Retain the ability to export ■ Consider local debt finance ■ Use offshore accounts to store hard currency ■ Pay large management fees to foreign stockholders to push money out of the country
Information Risk	■ Be prepared to conduct extra due diligence ■ Double-check company, industry, and macroeconomic data sources ■ Extend your investigative team past the normal Western disciplines

HOW SHOULD A WESTERN FIRM COMPENSATE FOR THE EXTRA RISK?

It's clear that an investment in an emerging market involves more risks—political, economic, currency, and information—than similar commitments in the developed world. The Western investors' first line of defense are the multiple structuring, selection and study alternatives discussed above, which serve to reduce the range of uncertainties.

A second line of defense is demanding a higher rate or return from the investment. The requisite amount of additional compensation is hard to quantify. As I noted earlier in the chapter, low-risk countries deserve lower return expectations than high-risk nations. The gradient of returns is set forth in Table 6.9, assuming

TABLE 6.9   Country Risk/Rate of Return Tradeoffs

	Minimum Expected Equity Rate of Return*
United States	12%–18%

Low-Risk Emerging Market
  Argentina
  Hungary
  Mexico
  South Korea
	15%–20%

Medium-Risk Emerging Market
  Columbia
  India
  Indonesia
  South Africa
	20%–30%

High-Risk Emerging Market
  Gambia
  Nicaragua
  Russia
  Vietnam
	30%–40%

*Lender's expected rate of returns are discussed in Chapter 9. Note how the riskier countries merit higher rates of return.

"Old Economy" service and manufacturing industries represent the investment candidates rather than high-tech concerns.

The matrix in Table 6.9 is a good guide, but investors take individual approaches. Hick Muse, the $8 billion equity, sorts countries by three risk categories, but "the particular characteristics of a deal in a given country are what defines the return," says John Civantos, a senior associate, "The business risk and the country environment in which the enterprise operates combine to define the level of uncertainty for which our investors should be compensated."

An executive at Enron, a major U.S. energy company, states, "our expected IRR depends on the country and type of investment. Emerging market countries require a higher hurdle rate, but the exact IRR target is also a function of the business. An electricity generation plant under a long-term sales contract is less risky than a gas exploration and production project."

Nonetheless, recent transactions indicate that my guideline IRR's are getting soft. "The first Westerners got into the emerging markets cheap," says Mike Heim, security analyst at A.G. Edwards, "as more people go in, it's a question of who has the dollars. Returns have dropped." This view is echoed by Massoud Mussavian, global emerging equity strategist at Credit Suisse First Boston, "In a recent study (May 2000), we tried to determine if emerging market stocks had a P/E discount to their peer groups in Western Europe. If you take out the growth differential, there's no real discount for emerging market risk." And a 1998 academic study by Tesar and Warner showed that the risk premium in emerging market stocks has dropped.

Many research analysts continue to make a distinction. At Edward Jones & Co., Zach Wagner, energy security analyst, thinks larger U.S. companies with emerging market exposure are reasonably priced, "On the price-earnings ratio, the discount for higher risk is essentially offset by the greater growth prospects. No further adjustment is required at this time (June 2000), but remember these markets are volatile." Specific comparisons sometimes highlight differentials. Both Calpine and AES are independent power producers

(IPP) headquartered in the United States. One hundred percent of Calpine's business is U.S.-based, while over one-half of AES' revenues come from the emerging markets. At June 2000, the consensus growth rate on both companies was 30 percent annually, yet, as indicated in Table 6.10, Calpine had a 52× P/E ratio, while AES had only a 30× P/E multiple. "The difference results from emerging market risk," says Ron Barone, IPP security analyst at PaineWebber, "AES pays a penalty for its exposure to developing countries, even though they do their best to mitigate the risk."

The volatility of the emerging markets affected AES' earnings and stock prices. In 1999, the Brazilian devaluation cost the company $203 million in foreign currency translation losses, and it resulted in net income for the year dropping by 27 percent, as compared to 1998's performance. Investors' worries about AES' commitment to

TABLE 6.10 Comparison of Two Independent Power Producer (IPP) Stocks

	Calpine	AES Corp.
Description	Calpine operates a diverse portfolio of electric power plants in the United States.	AES has electricity-generating plants in the United States and 16 other countries. Over 50% of its operations are based in the emerging markets.
Stock price	$60	$45
Estimated earnings per share in 2000	$1.15	$1.50
Price of earnings ratio	52×	30×
Expected annual growth rate	30%	30%
Discount on P/E multiple for emerging market exposure	No exposure	42%

Note: Both firms have 30 percent growth rates, but the P/E multiple of AES is lower due to its emerging market presence.

Brazil and similar economies pushed the stock price down by 50 percent in 1999, even as the stocks of Calpine and comparable firms advanced. The situation showed how investors discriminate against U.S. firms with a substantial exposure to the Third World.

Comparing a "pure" U.S. firm against same-industry operators in the emerging markets provides an illustration of how investors deal with risk. Table 6.11 shows the statistics of five cellular phone companies: two operate in the United States, two in China, and one in Russia. The Russian firm had the highest growth rate, but its equity valuation was 6 times revenues, less than the other four firms that traded at 8 times to 20 times revenues. I attributed the disparity to the perception that Russia had greater political and currency risk than either the United States or China. The Chinese firms had far better growth rates than the U.S. operators, and the markets rewarded them with premium Price to Sales ratios, despite the greater political risks. Note that China and Russia showed low "value per subscriber" ratios, in part due to the lower phone charges in those two countries, compared to the United States.

TABLE 6.11   Cellular Phone Company Valuation Data at June 2000

Country	Annual Growth Rate (%)	Company Market Value to Annual Sales (×)	Subscribers (Millions)	Company Market Value per Subscriber ($)
United States				
AT&T Wireless	60	8	12.0	4,500
Nextel	70	10	4.5	8,000
China				
China Telecom	100	20	25.0	5,000
China Unicom	80	12	4.2	5,500
Russia				
Mobile Telesystems	150	6	0.3	5,000

Note: Russia's higher growth rate didn't produce a higher valuation multiple. The perception of greater risk kept the multiple low.

SUMMARY

Emerging market investments are more risky than comparable opportunities in the developed world. Heightened levels of political, macro-economic, currency, and information risk are present in these regions, and Western investors demand a higher level of expected return. For a corporation that insists on a progressive, step-by-step performance from their investments, the emerging markets are inappropriate venues due to their inherent volatility.

CHAPTER 7

Portfolio Investment

In the prior chapters, we concentrated on strategic and operating investors—Western companies whose stake in the emerging market firm they buy is sufficient to give them control or influence in the running of the corporation. In this chapter, we consider the situation of the foreign portfolio investor. Such an investor does not have a sufficient ownership interest to influence corporate actions, even though his commitment can range from a few hundred shares to millions of dollars. Examples of portfolio investors are mutual funds, pension funds, insurance companies, private equity funds, hedge funds, and individuals. These investors buy securities that are either publicly-traded on a local exchange or listed on a Western exchange.

POPULARITY OF INTERNATIONAL INVESTING

The interest in emerging market equities is a subset of a larger trend toward the internationalization of stock market investing. Western institutions accept the idea of purchasing shares of companies headquartered outside of their home countries, and corporate securities are now quite accessible across borders. This situation mirrors the increasing globalization of the economy.

The popularity of international investing is also reflective of portfolio managers' desire to diversify a portion of their holdings out of domestic markets. In the United States, for example, mutual funds and pension plans continue to pour money into domestic stocks, so the dynamics of supply and demand ensure that the prices of many issues exceed historical markers. Some prudent managers hedge their bets and lay off a portion of their assets in foreign markets, where the risk/return tradeoff appears more favorable than that in the United States.

Besides the obvious diversification benefits, there is also the perception that foreign securities are not as efficiently priced as their Western counterparts. Regulatory barriers (such as governments forbidding insurance companies to invest in corporate shares) as well as the lack of local personnel with the requisite financial training contribute to this view. The presumed pricing inefficiencies leave opportunities for Wall Street analysts who are willing to perform the extra work required of an emerging market evaluation.

Also, many economies of developing countries are expanding faster than the First World economy. The implication is that rising GDP "top lines" translate into larger corporate "bottom lines." Since earnings growth is the main engine behind higher stock prices, it's easy to see why investors look to emerging markets. This being said, Table 7.1 indicates that most of the principal emerging market indices failed to keep pace with the S&P 500 over the 1990 to 2000 period.

BEGINNING OF WESTERN INTEREST IN EMERGING MARKET EQUITIES

Until the early 1990s, emerging market equity was a remote backwater of the investment industry. Blue-chip money managers and big-name institutions avoided these securities, and the business of analyzing, buying, and selling Third World shares was relegated to a small group of obscure hedge funds and brokerage houses.

Wall Street's initial exposure to the emerging markets was the defaulted debt securities of Latin American corporations and countries. The positioning and trading of this paper eventually led to corporate finance assignments in the region, and then to a search for business in other developing areas. As one example, during most of

TABLE 7.1 Compound Annual Performance of Emerging Stock Market Indices, 1990–2000

Country	Index
Argentina	22%
Brazil	33
China	(7)
India	(1)
Indonesia	(14)
Malaysia	(1)
Mexico	11
South Korea	(7)
Turkey	3
U.S. S&P 500	19
FT Europe	8

Note: US$ equivalent price appreciation and dividends. China, India, and South Korea indices start in 1992.

the 1990s, the head of emerging market investment banking for Bear Stearns & Co. was Stephen Cunningham, formerly a Latin American bond trader.

The piqued interest of Westerners coincided with a liberalization of investment regulations in certain markets, and foreign investors were able to place funds quickly on the local exchanges. By the early 1990s, the increasing flow of Western money chased a limited number of issues, and the sharp rise in demand propelled stock indices upward—far above comparable U.S. returns. Other investors spotted the trend—and allocated a portion of their portfolios to this new category. Their success precipitated another round of price increases, leading to a huge rise in the number of IPOs and secondary stock offerings that Westerners bought eagerly. Ridham Desai, security analyst at JM Morgan Stanley in Mumbai, India, echoed this view in a July 2000 research report, "Since January 1993, when foreign institutional investors (FII) were first allowed in India, their influence on equity markets has been evident. FIIs have led market behavior with

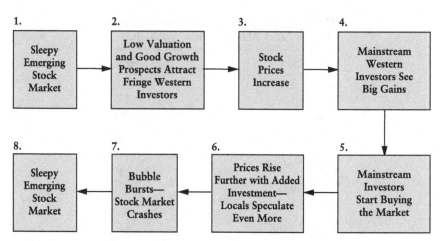

FIGURE 7.1   An illustration of how a flood of Western money boosts emerging market stock prices.

peak flows followed by market peaks and via versa." Academic papers by Froot, O'Connell, and Seasholes noticed a similar pattern. See Figure 7.1 for a sequencing of price increases and Figure 7.2 for a summary of price movements.

By the mid-1990s, "emerging markets" was in every asset allocator's lexicon. Institutions and individuals who didn't assign a small portion of their assets—say 3 percent to 5 percent—to the new category were considered behind the times. In just five years, Wall Street originated over 400 emerging market mutual funds to attract U.S. and European monies, collecting billions of dollars in the process. Encouraging this movement were three broad trends:

1. *Government deregulation.* Seeking foreign capital, governments eased foreign investment restrictions. (Most limited foreign ownership of publicly-traded firms.) Other obstacles to foreign investment, such as price controls, foreign exchange regulations, and legal barriers were loosened. Foreigners were invited into new areas such as cable-TV and wireless communication.

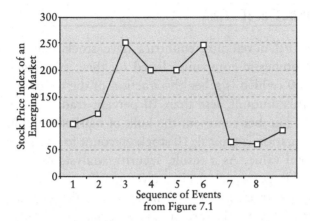

FIGURE 7.2   Tracing the flood of Western money and stock price index performance, Malaysia, 1991–1999.

2. *Privatization.* One-third of the largest emerging market firms resulted from 1990's privatizations. The biggest deals have been accomplished, but smaller privatizations continually create new listings.
3. *Globalization.* The rapid increase in telecommunications, trade, and transportation links the Third World more closely to the West.

As a new field, the emerging market investment business suffered from a dearth of experienced talent. No matter. Feeding the enthusiasm was a new breed of mostly young security analysts and fund managers who presented themselves as pathfinders in the uncharted terrain of the developing world. Speaking the requisite language of the exotic locales—Spanish, Russian, or Hindi, for example—became the first qualification for these new hires, and the requisite financial acumen occupied a secondary position. With only one or two years of experience in some cases, they were put in charge of recommending risky, complex, and volatile Third World securities. Such bull market excesses permitted questionable IPOs to come to market, and foreshadowed the lack of vigilance that contributed to later financial crises.

STOCK MARKET INVESTING

Today, over 70 developing countries have stock markets and the number of domestic companies listed on their exchanges approximates 25,000 (which is a healthy fraction of the developed country total). Of this amount, less than 10 percent trade actively, and an even smaller number represent the bulk of market capitalization. In India, the situation is typical; 10 stocks account for 30 percent of the market's total value. As a result, security analysts usually focus on just 20 to 30 large-cap stocks in a given market.

The stock markets are small compared with those of major industrial countries. China, the largest emerging market, is only 4 percent the size of the U.S. market, as indicated in Figure 7.3. Average daily turnover is only $2 billion, one-thirtieth of the U.S. total, and Hong Kong issues, rather than Mainland China stocks, represent two-thirds of the total. From a Westerner's standpoint, even these statistics are exaggerated, since foreigners are relegated to the sidelines. They're only permitted to purchase special "B shares" and only in a limited number of companies. The market capitalization of the B shares is less than one-twentieth of the Chinese market. Considering the restricted

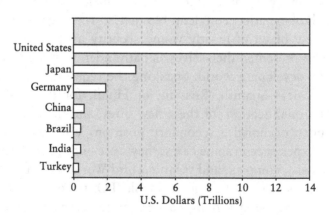

FIGURE 7.3   Comparative sizes of market capitalization.

liquidity of most Chinese stocks, the base of investment opportunities for investors in China is minuscule relative to that in the United States.

This environment of small capitalization, limited trading, and foreign ownership restriction is duplicated in other prominent emerging markets, including Argentina, Brazil, Chile, India, Indonesia, Malaysia, Mexico, Philippines, Thailand, and Turkey (see Figure 7.3). The entire Philippine stock market, for example, is worth less than Dupont, the U.S. chemical company. As a whole, the combined capitalization of all emerging stock markets is only 7 percent of global capitalization.

You have only to observe the stock exchanges of a few emerging markets to understand the vast differences between them and their developed country counterparts. As an investment executive for the IFC, I visited several stock exchanges in Latin America. The Medellin Stock Exchange in Colombia, for example, is a far cry from the image of the modern exchange (see Figure 7.5). Situated in a room that resembles an elementary school gymnasium, the Medellin Exchange is positively tranquil. Trading happens only two hours per day from 10 A.M. to

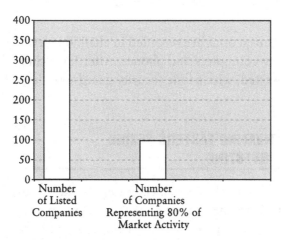

FIGURE 7.4 Typical emerging market.

FIGURE 7.5   Stock exchanges are frequently quiet places in the emerging markets, as shown in Medellin, Columbia.

noon, and transactions are recorded in chalk on elevated blackboards. There are few computers and phones. After lunchtime, the building is virtually deserted, with a lone security guard standing by the entrance.

INITIAL MOTIVATING FACTORS BEHIND PORTFOLIO INVESTING

In the beginning of the 1990s, emerging market securities were sold, not bought. With the default of Latin American governments in the early 1980s, commercial banks lost billions and institutional money managers remained leery. Brokerage firms had to be doubly convincing to get investors to take the extra risk involved with buying into poor countries.

For most investors, developing nations presented the image of starving children, dilapidated infrastructure and natural disasters. As part of its mission to stimulate Western interest, the World Bank Group did its part by inventing the term *emerging market* as a positive-sounding synonym for "Third World country." Rebounding economies, financial reforms, and the collapse of socialism reinforced the sales pitch.

As the scramble for creating a rational template for equity valuation ensured, Wall Street trotted out a four-legged stool. Brokerage firms said that emerging market stocks offered (1) diversification, (2) countercyclical behavior, (3) higher growth, and (4) better returns, all as compared to a U.S. stock portfolio. Like many sales schemes, there was little evidence behind these arguments, and these claims turned out to be either false or exaggerated (see Table 7.2).

Diversification

Theoretically, opening up a Western portfolio to emerging market stocks brings immediate diversification opportunities since the number of possible investee companies doubles. However, only about 250 emerging market stocks have market caps exceeding $1 billion, which is the minimum for most U.S. institutions, and even this figure is overstated since the majority of the stock is closely held, rather than freely-traded. The vast majority of the new stock selections have small floats, thus limiting the ability of the portfolio manage to commit funds and realize true diversification. Patel, Sarkar, and Wang commented that the diversification benefits were slim at best. Robert Hrabchak, portfolio manger at Warburg Pincus Asia, summarizes the situation, "There are some good companies there, but it's too difficult to take a meaningful position."

TABLE 7.2   Emerging Market Portfolio Investing, Motivations versus Myths

Motivation	Myth
1. *Diversification.* Buying the shares of emerging market companies broadens the investment universe and further diversification.	This is largely true, but the small size of these markets limits such benefits.
2. *Counter cyclical.* According to many promoters, emerging stock market movements didn't correlate well with Western indices. Thus, the markets offer a hedge against adverse fluctuations in the United Sates and Europe.	Not proven over the long-term.
3. *Higher growth.* Emerging market firms provide higher earnings growth than their Western counterparts.	This supposition is true only in certain cases. The "boom-and-bust" cycles dilute the higher growth concept.
4. *Higher returns.* Pricing inefficiencies provide Western investors with better returns relative to their home markets.	Academic research suggests that the emerging markets' results don't beat Western equity indices.

Countercyclicality

Academic studies show that emerging stock markets have a low covariance with the developed stock markets. In other words, the evidence suggests countercyclical behavior. "The problem with this body of work," suggests Bill Goetzman, finance professor at Yale University, "is that the data is generally accurate only from 1980 to the present time, when the IFC began preparing emerging market price indices. Going further back, you don't see the benefits of the covariance. Historically, when global markets suffer, interest in emerging markets disappears with the investors' flight to quality. Portfolio capital retreats from these markets in a dramatic fashion." Michael Barth and Xin Zhang of the World Bank note that Asian markets strongly correlated with U.S. markets during U.S. crisis periods, which is the opposite of countercyclicality.

Higher Growth

The case that emerging market companies uniformly deliver higher earnings growth rates than their Western counterparts is not supported by the facts. In certain countries, this supposition holds true over selected periods, but the boom-and-bust cycles of these economies contradict the substance of the generalization, as corporate earnings dry up during hard times. Jonathan Garner and Alex Redman of Donaldson, Lufkin & Jenrette, a major brokerage firm, commented on the weak link between demand growth and local corporate earnings. They pointed out how emerging market airline and telecommunication firms didn't convert sharp revenue increases into matching stock performance.

Higher Returns

In the early 1990s, the shortage of Western professionals in these markets produced the notion that the stocks were inefficiently priced, producing the chance for above-average returns. At the same time, the higher volatility of the markets suggested higher returns, as long as investors stayed in for extended periods. Chris Barry, professor at Texas Christian University, concluded that these stocks don't consistently provide higher returns over varying time periods. While the past is not always the best predictor of the future—and much has changed in the developing world—the ease with which this myth was disproven indicates added caution before a portfolio commitment is made. (See Table 7.3.)

SECURITY ANALYSIS AND THE EMERGING MARKETS

As the author of *Security Analysis on Wall Street* (New York: Wiley, 1998), I like to say the pricing of U.S. stocks is 50 percent economic logic and 50 percent emotion. The logical portion of this equation stems from the field of study known as security analysis, which

TABLE 7.3 Performance of Emerging Market Stock
Markets—Total Return Statistics

Emerging Market	Five Years Ended February 2001 Total Return Performance (%)
Argentina	+23
Brazil	+50
Chile	−14
India	−1
Indonesia	−84
Malaysia	−62
Mexico	+64
Thailand	−86
Turkey	+27
United States	+139

Note: US$ price appreciation and dividend payments. The
principal emerging markets underperformed the U.S. indices.

maintains that stocks can be valued in a methodical and sensible
way. Important determinants to a reasonable valuation are the health
of a company's business, its future prospects, overriding industry and
economic concerns, and the relative pricing of alternative investments. Thousands of people in the United States work as full-time security analysts. Fidelity, the mutual fund giant, has over 200 analysts
on staff. Merrill Lynch, the largest brokerage house, employs over
250 analysts.

As emerging markets play a larger role in Western portfolios, practitioners gradually apply conventional security analysis to these exotic
stocks. They write long research reports, complete financial projections, and compare relative values. Despite such attempts at rational
analysis, the approach is valid only in a handful of the more advanced
countries, and perhaps with just a few of the dominant stocks in the
lesser markets. For the most part, share valuations remain the subject
of speculation and momentum investing. Consider the remarks of
Peter Alexander, who works for Direct Pacific Financial Services, a
Shanghai-based brokerage firm. Commenting on the wild gyrations
in China's stock market, he said, "Compare it to an OTB (off track

betting) parlor at 42nd Street and Sixth Avenue (in New York). There are people staring at a huge screen; there's some guy crying in the corner that he just blew his daughter's college tuition, and the boss is in the back counting all the money. Exactly the same."

Michael Pomerleano and Xin Zhang of the World Bank indicate that Western methods are at a loss to describe developing market valuation. They suggest that emerging markets do not price risk adequately and the investment style is speculative. Other academics, such as Lakonishok, Shreifer, Vishny, and Haugen notice deviations from the standard risk-return paradigm. One interpretation of their findings is that emerging markets are dominated by "naïve" investors who equate *quality companies* with *quality stocks*. Thus, Brazilians buy TeleCabo, the largest cable-television firm, at $9,000 per subscriber because they've heard of the firm, while Canbras, a smaller cable-television firm with a similar growth story, trades at $1,200 per subscriber. Another example is seen in China, where retail investors consider low-priced stocks as "value plays." A $1 stock is therefore a better buy than a $2 stock, no matter what either company's business prospects are.

A gambling mentality prevails in these markets, and the serious investor who isn't willing to dedicate a full-time effort is better off participating in a country fund that more or less "indexes" a given market. Even savvy investors such as ING Emerging Markets Investors (EMI) emphasize the country approach, rather than picking individual stocks. According to Scott Gordon, an EMI portfolio manager, "We tend to express a broad view on a market rather than a view of stock or company's performance." He cites studies that indicate that picking the right emerging market country has been a much more important criteria than picking the right stocks.

PRACTICAL PROBLEMS WITH RATIONAL ANALYSIS OF EMERGING MARKET EQUITIES

The analytical process for Western portfolio managers is heavily reliant on informed decisions. Not only must the data for a research study be available and reliable, but the prices of comparable securities must be based on open and honest trading. Such standards are usually met in the United States, assuming the analyst makes a determined research effort, but achieving the desired result in an emerging market is problematic. The developing markets have various degrees of shortcomings, including:

1. Less information.
2. Questionable trading practices.
3. Unclear accounting standards.
4. Few comparables.
5. Reduced emphasis on share price enhancement.
6. Liquidity concerns.
7. Uncertain registration, settlement, clearing, and custodial systems.
8. Minority rights.

Less Information

Regulators and exchanges require less corporate disclosure than their U.S. counterparts. That information which is submitted by issuers faces little official scrutiny. Depending on the country, the availability and accuracy of macroeconomic, capital market, and industry data are also suspect. Moreover, much of the source material is not translated into English. For the security analyst, less information means more guesswork.

Emerging market companies are lax in reporting events affecting their respective businesses, and they release financial results in an untimely fashion. If the corporation is controlled by a founding family, the managers (who usually are family members) are reluctant to provide information to the public and meet with analysts, citing competitive reasons.

Notable exceptions to this behavior are the emerging market companies that have American Depository Receipts (ADRs) listed in the United States. They adhere to stock exchange standards on disclosure, and the management is more forthcoming in taking analysts' questions.

Questionable Trading Practices

Insider trading, front-running, poor execution, and other unsavory practices are common on emerging market exchanges. To some, the situation is reminiscent of the U.S. market's lack of regulation in the early 1900s. Charles Randolph of KPMG Peat Marwich summarized the problem in the Czech Republic, "One of the biggest complaints of the Czech financial markets has been not that there's a lack of laws on the books, but rather there's a lack of enforcement." Although such practices are regrettable, for now foreign investors in these markets consider them a cost of doing business.

In late 1998, a few months after I had closed a $40 million equity investment with Hankook Synthetic, a Korean chemical manufacturer, the company decided to issue US$ 43 million (equivalent) of convertible bonds on the Seoul exchange. Two weeks before the bonds' pricing, Hankook's shares began a steady climb, increasing in value by over 50 percent on no real news. It was clear that management manipulated the price to cut the dilutive impact of the new issue. Shortly after the convertible deal closed, the shares quickly retreated to prior levels.

Unclear Accounting Standards

A basic methodology in security analysis is comparing the merits of one company against a similar firm operating in the same business. This process requires consistent accounting methods. Otherwise, the analyst compares "apples to oranges." The variety of accounting regimes in the developing world and the differing manner of application present the analyst with a challenge in interpreting financial results and estimating a company's current earnings power. The difficulties increases as you go down the corporate status chain (see Table 7.4).

The large firms that list their ADRs in the United States adhere to the strictest accounting certification and presentation. Furthermore, they show their results in U.S. dollar equivalent and provide U.S. GAAP translations. The remaining blue chip firms, numbering from

20 to 30 companies in an emerging market, release financial statements that are usually a fair representation of the economic results of their respective businesses. Nevertheless, the practitioner needs to examine these statements with a great deal of care and to ask management pointed questions that uncover well-hidden deficiencies. One Mexican firm I visited papered over operating losses by buying small businesses at prices below book value. The company then wrote up the assets and realized a gain; this was permitted by the firm's independent auditor.

As the investor proceeds to the second-tier firms that make up 40 percent to 50 percent of an emerging market's capitalization, the accounting shenanigans increase. At many such firms, an important objective is minimizing asset, value-added, and income taxes. As a result, perhaps 10 percent to 30 percent of sales go unreported and the tax burden is commensurately reduced. Furthermore, the majority of second-tier companies are family affairs, so there is little hesitation in placing personal charges on the books, obviously at the expense of outside shareholders. Also, transfer pricing between the family companies is frequently an undisclosed issue. If the publicly-traded pulp producer purchases its lumber from the family's privately-owned timber operation, the price of that timber should be a matter of public record. Local regulations require that listed companies have their books audited by an independent accounting firm (or designated auditor), but emerging market accountants often turn a blind eye to these practices or simply fail to perform the necessary investigations.

Regulators around the world have been looking for ways to standardize accounting methods. In May 2000, Paul Volcker, former head of the Federal Reserve Bank was named to head a group that will try to create an enforceable set of international accounting standards. The task will not be simple because many countries and companies have a vested interest in continuing past practices, and most countries lack the enforcement power to make new regulations meaningful (see Table 7.4).

The majority of investment books and research reports on emerging markets fail to publicize these accounting problems. This

TABLE 7.4 Emerging Market Companies—Quality of Accounting Disclosure

Companies with ADRs listed in the United States	High-standard of disclosure. Accurate audits with supplementary presentation in U.S. GAAP.
Other first-tier emerging market companies	Financial statements provide a reasonably fair presentation of economic result. The analyst must still conduct a thorough study to estimate current earnings power.
Second-tier firms	Publicly-disclosed accounting results are suspect. Income tax avoidance and family enrichment are normal practices. Foreign investors should seek an extra margin of safety.

deficiency highlights the need for more study of these frontier markets, before the average investor takes the plunge.

Few Comparables

The U.S. market is so large that almost every public company has a few "comparables." As one proceeds to smaller economies, the number of comparables decreases rapidly. Practitioners compensate for this shortage by comparing similar firms across national boundaries. A telephone company stock in Thailand is evaluated against one in another developing country, such as Indonesia, India, or Poland. Given different country environments and variable accounting systems, this approach has apparent weaknesses.

Reduced Emphasis on Share Price Enhancement

The preponderance of emerging market companies are controlled by their respective founding families. Therein lies the fundamental conflict between listed firms and their outside shareholders. Families are not driven to maximize value for the benefit of outside shareholders. Rather, the emphasis is on keeping the family executives in power, so they can preserve their status and influence within the community. This represents an important philosophical difference from U.S.-style investors, who want to see an issuer pursue aggressive tactics that boost its share price.

The "family-first" attitude is manifested in several ways. One, the company may pass on promising growth opportunities if the resultant financing requirement means ownership dilution. Two, the firm may display a marked preference for family executives, as opposed to hiring skilled outside management. And three, it may permit the family's enrichment (through personal prerequisites or insider deals) at the expense of the passive outside shareholder. Table 7.5 summarizes these issues.

An extension of the family control is the use of interlocking directorates and cross shareholdings. These protect management from hostile investors. Widely known as *chaebols* in Korea, for example, these arrangements are popular throughout Asia, are extensively used in parts of Latin America, and are achieving acceptance in Russia. The Ayala group in the Philippines is a perfect example of this phenomenon, as illustrated in Figure 7.6.

As Western institutions play a larger role in the emerging markets, the family-first preoccupation is likely to diminish. In the meantime,

TABLE 7.5 Family Influence in Emerging Market Stocks

The family-controlled firm often:
- Is not driven to maximize shareholder value.
- Is reluctant to meet with analysts and provide information.
- Prefers family executives to professional managers.
- Sacrifices growth opportunities to avoid shareholder dilution.
- Permits improper insider arrangements.
- Stresses income tax avoidance instead of complete financial reporting.

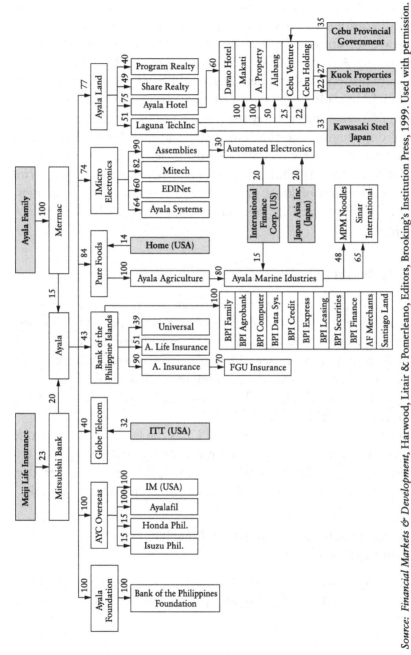

Source: Financial Markets & Development, Harwood, Litair & Pomerleano, Editors, Brooking's Institution Press, 1999. Used with permission.

FIGURE 7.6   Ownership structure of the Ayala Group, the Phillipines.

investors who want to minimize the problem should focus on public privatizations and new technology businesses. Public privatizations are businesses that were formerly owned by the local government. As a result, there is no founding family and ownership is usually dispersed. Prominent shareholders of these privatizations often include multinationals that believe in creating value quickly. Of the 250 emerging market firms with public capitalizations over $1 billion, roughly one-third are privatizations that occurred over the last 10 years. New technology businesses in the emerging markets, such as cellular phones or cable television, are commonly run by a combination of local investors and international companies. The latter share the U.S. portfolio manager's penchant for near-term gains.

Liquidity Concerns

Large institutional investors prefer stocks that trade actively so that they can move in and out of investments reasonably quickly. With the exception of a couple of hundred stocks, most listed firms have small floats. Even if an investor sees a bargain, he may have difficulty profiting from his efforts, because anything more than a token buying effort boosts the stock price. This discourages large institutions from making substantial commitments.

For example, Shin Corporation, PCL is the largest cellular phone company in Thailand, but on an average day, it trades only 200,000 shares. At current levels, that's only $1 million in value per day, which is too low for the large Western funds to participate actively.

Uncertain Registration, Settlement, Clearing, and Custodial Systems

In the smaller emerging markets, investors face registration, settlement, and custody risks in purchasing and selling securities; these risks are not normally recognized in more developed markets. In certain countries, securities are evidenced in book entry form rather than physical share certificates, heightening the risk of management shenanigans. Systems for clearing trades of securities are improving, but the uncertainties in the clearing and settlement process pose risks and delays.

Minority Rights

An old Wall Street saying is "a minority stockholder is the loneliest person in the world." This saying comes up in spades in the developing world, where minority stockholders—such as portfolio investors—have fewer rights than in the United States. The ability to influence management (or controlling shareholder) action is minimal, and investors protesting unfair treatment have little recourse, as practical matter, except to sell.

The notion that management and board members have a fiduciary obligation to represent all shareholders is not well advanced in the developing world. Below-market product sales, asset stripping, and sweetheart contracts are not uncommon perks for the controlling stockholders of publicly-traded firms. Abuses are common, and the policing system is ineffective. With increased exposure to Western investors, the notion of accountability to all shareholders gains wider acceptance but changes, particularly in the smaller markets, is slow in coming.

HOW TO SOLVE THE PROBLEMS?

It is clear the investment banking firms and their attorneys are aware of the risks for portfolio investors. That's why the June 2000 initial public offering prospectus of Mobile Telesystems OJSC, a Russian cellular phone company, mentioned 63 separate investment risks spread over an astounding 23 pages of text! U.S. IPOs—even the most speculative technology deals—come with a lot less baggage.

The best antidote for the Western portfolio investor in dealing with these issues is demanding a higher return. If a selection of U.S. stocks is expected to provide a 15 percent IRR, than a collection of Eastern European equities, for example, should have an expected return of 20 percent to 25 percent.

INVESTMENT ALTERNATIVES

Portfolio investors play the emerging markets in several ways:

- Mutual funds.
- Depository receipts.
- Direct purchase of local shares.
- Private equity funds.

Mutual Funds

For individuals, most of the larger mutual fund groups offer an emerging market product. The assortment of funds is broad, covering global funds, regional funds, country funds, and specialized industry funds. In an institutional setting, asset management firms such as Mercury, Capital Research, and Alliance Capital Management provide similar alternatives for pension funds and university endowments.

Within the mutual fund category are the index funds. Such funds copy country, regional, or global indices prepared by either Morgan Stanley Dean Wittier or International Finance Corporation.

Depository Receipts

For investors who wish to select their own stocks, depository receipts are a good start. These receipts are negotiable certificates

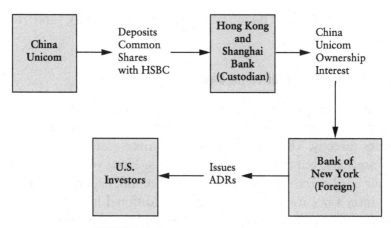

FIGURE 7.7 Depository receipts.

that represent a company's publicly-traded equity, and they are traded on Western stock exchanges. The receipts are created when a broker purchases the company's shares on the home stock market and delivers the shares to the depository's local custodian bank, which then instructs the foreign bank to issue depository receipts (see Figure 7.7).

Depository receipts are bought and sold in hard currency, outside of the home country. The legal structure of the certificates means foreign ADR buyers avoid the taxes and fees that are involved in trading stocks on the local exchange.

Two common forms of depository receipts are American depository receipts (ADRs) and global depository receipts (GDRs). Both ADRs and GDRs are public issues. They are issued as a sponsored Level I, that is, over the counter, or as a sponsored Level II, which allows the depository receipt to be traded on an exchange. To achieve Level II status, the issuing firm must comply with U.S. accounting principles. ADRs are becoming more popular with investors and issuers. By way of example, over 40 Brazilian ADRs trade on the U.S. markets. Prominent companies with ADRs include Telefonos de Mexico,

China UNICOM, Banco de Galicia (Argentina), and Telebras (Brazil).

Direct Purchases of Local Shares

Many developing countries allow individuals and institutions to open local brokerage accounts, whereby they can buy and sell securities directly. This option opens the universe of non-ADR stocks to Westerners, but it has a few drawbacks. First, you'll have to change your hard currency into local money. Second, depending on the local country's tax treaties, there may be additional income tax exposure for the foreign investors. Major U.S. banks and brokerage firms can make helpful suggestions about selecting overseas brokers that can assist you in this process.

Private Equity Funds

Private equity funds acquire large ownership positions in companies through privately negotiated transactions, usually involving $10 million or more. A staple of the American investment scene over the last 15 years, they're making modest inroads into the emerging markets. The largest collection of such funds, totaling $4 billion of assets, is managed by Emerging Markets Partnership of Washington DC, where I worked prior to starting my consulting business.

STOCK SELECTION GUIDELINES

In the typical emerging market, the quasi-scientific investors who rely on discounted cash flow and relative value techniques are greatly outnumbered by the speculators and momentum investors. As a result, the pricing of a stock often has little relation to its perceived economic value, as calculated using Western methodologies. These discrepancies present interesting investment opportunities (both on the long and short side), but the time it takes for the market to correct itself is sometimes prolonged, relative to the time needed for inefficiencies in the United States to resolve themselves. Veteran professionals acknowledge the situation and urge investors to consider the long-term perspective.

Mark Mobius, director of the Templeton Funds' global research effort, summarized the long-term philosophy

Taking a long view of emerging markets will yield excellent results for the investor prepared to be patient and willing to apply sound and tested principles in a diligent and consistent manner. The approach we take in our reports is not to focus on the short-term since we invest the funds entrusted to us not for a three-month, six-month or even one-year period, but for at least a five-year period. Over the many years that Templeton Funds have been investing, we have found that striving for short-term performance increases the risks to the shareholders and actually results in poorer returns. Only by taking the long view will we be able to do the best job for investors.

The speculative nature of these markets means they lurch from one valuation extreme to another (not unlike certain sectors of the U.S. hi-tech market). An investor can buy a Pakistani stock at 500 rupees per share, believing its intrinsic value is 700 rupees. However, if market sentiment becomes negative, the stock price can easily drop 30 percent (to 350 rupees) in a few weeks. Even though the margin of safety has widened to 50 percent, it takes an investor with a strong stomach to "double-up" at the lower price. He's never quite sure when the crash will bottom out. Figure 7.8 illustrates the volatility of several large markets.

Institutional investors tend to favor a methodical approach to evaluating common stocks. This process begins with a review of the relevant country's economic environment and extends through company-specific analysis and financial projections. The sequential study is referred to as the top-down approach, and its logic essentially says, "if the Peruvian economy is going to hell, then most Peruvian stocks are going to be poor investments." Table 7.6 summarizes

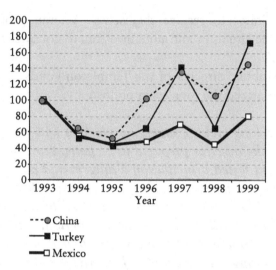

FIGURE 7.8 The emerging market roller coaster (in U.S.$ equivalents). Similar patterns are evident in U.S. Internet and biotech stocks.

TABLE 7.6 Top-Down Approach to Evaluating Common Stocks

Step 1	Macroeconomic Review	How is the local economy performing? What are the expectations?
Step 2	Capital Markets	Where are the stock markets heading? What is the outlook on interest rates?
Step 3	Industry Analysis	What is the industry forecast of the target company? Is competition increasing? What's the prognosis for growth?
Step 4	Company Analysis	In light of the above conclusions, what are the expectations for the company's future sales and profits?

TABLE 7.7   Emerging Markets—Stock Selection Guidelines

A few guidelines to follow in buying an emerging market stock include:

Country
- Reasonably stable economic indicators
- Moderate political risk

Capital Markets
- Semblance of fair trading and honest disclosure
- Sensible degree of liquidity

Industry
- Good growth prospects
- Internationally competitive
- Profits not reliant on tariffs, quotas, or other trade barriers

Company
- Modern management techniques
- Widely held ownership or influential multinational shareholder that promotes share price enhancement
- Strong government connections through family or management
- Good track record and solid balance sheet
- Growth prospects are favorable
- Purchase price is significantly below economic value

the methodology. In the next few paragraphs, we cover selection guidelines for the four segments of the top-down approach (see Table 7.7).

Country

As we discussed earlier, most emerging markets lack an independent central bank. Economic stability is compromised by capricious government policies, and legislators fail to appreciate the benefits of strong financial markets. In contrast, foreign investors seek a stable country in both a political and economic sense. (Exceptions are made for companies that deal primarily in export industries, such as gold mining or oil exploration, where revenues are generated in a hard currency like the U.S. dollar.) Besides macroeconomic matters, foreign investors assess the likelihood of government interference with their equity investment. Defined as political risk, these actions include foreign exchange blockage, legal discrimination, and expropriation. The Hungarian government enticed Western investors into the electric utility industry by promising to raise electricity prices by 35 percent. When the time came to implement the tariff increase, the government reneged, fearing riots in the streets. After intense investor pressure, the government pushed through a 24 percent increase. Political action reduced investor returns.

Capital Markets

Since few stocks move against the general trend in an emerging market, the investor needs to be confident of the market's upward direction (or downward move, in the case of a short sale). Additionally, a minimal standard of fair trading and honest disclosure is a strong plus for the portfolio participant.

Industry

The primary focus of the foreign portfolio investor is finding local industries with good growth prospects. As noted earlier, certain industries considered stodgy in the United Sates are considered hot in the emerging stock markets. One illustration is the electric utility industry. In the United States, this industry is mature; unit sales growth is only 2 percent to 3 percent annually. In contrast, electricity demand growth can be 2 to 3 times this rate in a market such as Brazil, because advancing prosperity means more electronic conveniences and appliances. The same can be said for the old-fashioned wireline phone company. The United States, with 65 lines per 100 residents, is saturated for conventional phones, but in the emerging markets, the average family doesn't have a phone. Thus, Peru's phone industry, with an average of 7 phones per 100 residents, can experience 10 years of 10 percent unit growth, and the country will still remain far below saturation level. Ninety-nine percent of the emphasis is on "Old Economy" type firms, because the emerging markets lack the infrastructure to support technological innovation.

To ensure long-term shareholder returns, the local industry has to be cost competitive, or substitute providers enter the market. Determining the economic efficiency of a local industry, and the magnitude of this threat, is a challenge. In many emerging markets, local industries are protected against foreign competition by high tariffs, import quotas, or obtrusive regulations. Because of the artificial pricing environment, a local industry that is inefficient by international cost standards can generate consistent profits. The textile industry in Colombia, for example, survived for years using outdated methods; eventually, extensive smuggling from India and Bangladesh crippled local producers.

Alternatively, the artificial environment enables the local industry to charge oligopolistic prices, thus providing excess profits and the image of premium economic returns. Brazil initially issued one cable-television license per municipality, as a way of kick-starting the cable-television industry. Early entrants enjoyed monopoly pricing power, which will fade as the government permits a second license in these areas. Despite 1996 legislation to promote competition, Telmex uses its local service monopoly to undercut long distance rivals in Mexico. Five years later, the company's network service charges are six times the rates charged in Chile.

Depending on the nature of the protections, the analyst must determine whether they represent a sustainable competitive advantage. Does the industry have enough influence with the government (and with future governments) to maintain the status quo? If the answer is no, the analyst must assess the likelihood and timing of a rollback of the protections. For example, the Mexican cement industry enjoyed import protection through numerous administrations. The Mexican packaged food industry, however, never had this benefit.

The practitioner must also consider the investment required by industry participants to fight off international competitors. More investment means fewer dividends and more share issuances, translating into lower share prices.

If the industry's international advantage is readily apparent—such as cheap labor—the analyst wants to be sure of the duration of that advantage. Relatively high wages in Singapore sent low-tech assembly industries to lower wage Malaysia. Now, as Malaysian salaries increase, the jobs are shipped to Indonesia. Paul Ziegler, Asian CEO for Asea Brown Boveri, the Swedish power equipment manufacturer, said, "It's just common sense. You make these things where they are cheapest to make," noting that labor costing his company the equivalent of $10 in Singapore can be obtained for $3 in Malaysia and just $1.60 in Indonesia.

Company

The company selection process incorporates appraisal techniques that are similar to those discussed in *Security Analysis on Wall Street* (Wiley, 1998), *Security Analysis* (McGraw-Hill, 1962), and other investment books. Good growth prospects, a solid balance sheet, Western-style management, and enlightened owners are especially notable for emerging market companies. Furthermore, because of the heavy government influence and arbitrary regulation that characterize these economies, a firm with close ties to the ruling party is a good bet. Since governments come and go in these countries, political influence can wane, so it is important that the firm selected for investment have intrinsic competitive qualities. Helmut Paul, who administered the International Finance Corporation's vast Latin American portfolio, explains, "In today's global arena, it's not enough for an emerging market company to be excellent by country or by regional standards; it must be competitive by world standards. And a good distribution system or local brand name is not sufficient; these can be duplicated by international competition."

SUMMARY

Emerging markets represent a standard allocation category for large institutional investors. Dominated by speculative elements, these volatile markets provide good investment opportunities, but the bottom line is that U.S.-style research techniques don't travel well. The lack of information, poor regulatory environment, and illiquidity conspire to frustrate investors using Western methodologies.

Furthermore, the pattern of actual trading suggests that traditional stock pricing takes a backseat to sovereign concerns. Investors ignore the important distinctions among individual stocks, focusing instead on countries as a whole. This behavior makes for inefficient pricing, but the portfolio manager relying on fundamental analysis to earn premium returns must be prepared to ride out the speculative waves. As a result, only investors with a strong stomach should pursue these markets.

CHAPTER 8

Valuation Case Study

In Chapter 7, we covered the two principal approaches used by Western investors to value common stocks:

1. *Intrinsic value.* A business is worth the net present value of its dividends. Sooner or later, a business will trade at its intrinsic value, justifying investment decisions made on that basis.
2. *Relative value.* Determine a company's value by comparing it to similar companies' values. If one company's pricing is out of line with its peer group, eventually market forces will push the pricing toward fair value.

Emerging market equity valuations are driven heavily by speculation, and the two quasi-scientific methodologies receive less attention than they do in New York or London. Aware of this limitation, I apply each valuation technique in this chapter to a prominent Brazilian company, Industrias Klabin de Papel e Celulose, S.A. (referred to as Klabin or the Company).

CORPORATE OVERVIEW

Klabin is a packaging, pulp, and pulp manufacturer based in São Paulo, Brazil. Sixty-five percent of sales are made to the domestic market and 35 percent of sales are represented by exports, principally to other South American nations. Before financial expenses and

TABLE 8.1 Klabin Summary Financial Data (in Millions of Brazilian Reals)

| Income Statement | Year Ended December 31 | | | 5-Year Compound Annual Growth Rate |
	1997	1998	1999	
Net Sales	Rs. 1,153	Rs. 1,106	Rs. 1,482	2%
EBITDA	226	181	457	7
Operating profit	72	33	312	21
Net income	(4)	(34)	(116)	na
Earnings per ADR	(0.05)	(0.44)	(1.55)	na

Balance Sheet	At December 31, 1999
Cash	Rs. 281
Fixed assets	2,030
Total assets	3,189
Total debt	1,632
Stockholders' equity	1,016

devaluation costs, Klabin is consistently profitable and its balance sheet is conservatively leveraged. Internal family disputes have hindered progress and the retention of professional management, but the overall trend is positive. Reported financial data for the three years ended December 31, 1999 are set forth in Table 8.1.

Inflation and devaluations tend to distort the financial statements of emerging market issuers. As a result, Western investors prefer to translate the results into U.S. dollar equivalents. Income statement data is translated at average exchange rates while balance sheet information is translated at year-end rates. (See Table 8.2 for a U.S. dollar translation.)

SUMMARY TOP-DOWN ANALYSIS

A proper top-down study easily fills 20 to 30 pages in a typed format. For the sake of illustration, I only present a few remarks

TABLE 8.2 Klabin Summary Financial and Market Data (in Millions of U.S. Dollar-Equivalents, Except per Share Data and Percentages)

Income Statement	Year Ended December 31			5-Year Compound Annual Growth Rate
	1997	1998	1999	
Net sales	US$ 1,067	US$ 953	US$ 814	(6)%
EBITDA	209	156	251	(1)
Operating profit	67	28	171	9
Net income	(4)	(29)	(64)	na
Earnings per ADR	(0.05)	(0.38)	(0.87)	na

Balance Sheet	At December 31, 1999
Cash	US$ 157
Fixed assets	1,135
Total assets	1,783
Total debt	912
Stockholders' equity	568

Market Data	At June 30, 2000
Klabin ADR price[a]	US$ 9.58
P/E multiple[b]	5.0x
Price/book value	1.0x
Enterprise value/EBITDA[c]	3.8x
Dividend yield	1.6%

[a] ADR represents 10 shares.
[b] Based on 2000 estimated EPS.
[c] Based on 2000 estimated EBITDA.

regarding (1) the study's conclusions and (2) the assumptions for the financial projections.

Macroeconomy

Brazil suffered a devaluation and flat economic growth in 1999. Inflation rose as the devaluation increased import costs, but it will moderate over time. Following the emerging market pattern after such events, an economic rebound is forecast from 2000 to 2003, followed by another recession in 2004:

	1998	1999	2000 (E)	2001 (P)
Real GDP growth (%)	0.1	0.0	3.1	3.9
Consumer price inflation (%)	1.7	9.0	7.9	6.3
Average exchange rate (real: US$)	1.16	1.82	1.86	1.90

With a GNP per capita of $4,790, Brazil ranks third in Latin America behind Argentina ($8,950) and Chile ($4,820).

Capital Markets

Forecasting the Brazilian stock and bond markets is a hazardous exercise. This case assumes a moderate upward trend in share prices, responding to the growth in corporate earnings and a slight rise in Brazilian P/E ratios. P/E and EBITDA multiples for the packaging, pulp and paper industries fluctuate within previous limits.

Industry

The Brazilian packing pulp and paper industry is concentrated among several major producers, and Klabin is the largest paper manufacturer and second largest pulp maker. Low production costs and plentiful forests make the industry a net exporter. The 1999 devaluation strengthened the Company's export abilities by making production expenses lower in U.S. dollar terms.

In Brazil, packaging, pulp, and paper prices are closely tied to consumer spending. With the 1998–1999 recession, discretionary spending was curtailed, hurting the consumption rate of Klabin's products. Over the last three years, Brazil paper consumption only increased 9 percent. Klabin's unit volume in 1999 was only 3 percent higher than 1998's result, and without additional export sales, 1999 unit volume would have dropped. (See Table 8.3 on page 163.)

Packaging and paper consumption is directly related to per capita GDP levels, and Brazil's per capita consumption is a fraction of the United States' usage. As Brazil's GDP climbs, the demand for Klabin's products will increase steadily.

The international paper market is closely linked to the health of the global economy. The economic crisis in Asia disrupted the global demand for paper, and product prices suffered as a result. As Asian demand recovers and production capacity stagnate, demand and supply should obtain a better balance, thereby pushing prices upward.

The Company

The Company has dominant positions in its principal markets. In Brazil, it is the largest paper manufacturer, second largest pulp maker, and the leader in 10 out of its 11 packaging product lines. The Company has an excellent reputation for product quality and fair dealings, and its majority owner is the Klabin family, which has been well-established in Brazilian business circles for decades. Highly regarded in the Western financial community, Klabin has sold four separate Eurobonds (totaling $230 million) to institutional investors in the United States and Europe. Operational data is set forth in Table 8.3.

TABLE 8.3 Klabin's Operational Data (in Thousands of Metric Tons)

	1997	1998	1999
Total shipments	1,274	1,316	1,355
Corrugated boxes	262	282	307
Tissue	128	141	133
Packaging paper	265	248	289
Market pulp	251	265	274
Dissolving pulp	89	105	104
Newsprint	111	112	88
Sacks and envelopes	92	99	101
Exports as percent of shipments	34%	32%	35%

Historical Financial Analysis

As Table 8.2 illustrates, the Company's growth rate in a "hard currency" translation (i.e., minus 6 percent in US$) is far lower than the Brazilian performance (plus 2 percent, see Table 8.1). Part of the difference reflected the lower value given local sales as the Brazilian currency depreciated against the U.S. dollar. The remainder resulted from (1) Brazil's economic problems, and (2) cyclically low paper prices that hurt the Company's results in 1997 and 1998. After the 1999 devaluation, Brazil's economy started to recover, increasing the demand for Klabin's products. Concurrently, the global cycle for paper prices turned around, providing better profit margins.

Financial Projections

Security analysis uses three projection techniques:

1. *Time series.* This method suggests that the future will be like the past. It is well suited for basic industries such as food, brewing, and electricity.
2. *Causal.* The causal techniques forecast results by establishing relationships between corporate sales and certain external variables, such as housing starts or interest rates. Supermarket sales, for example, are dependent on population growth, among other factors.
3. *Qualitative.* Qualitative projection techniques are applied to pioneer companies, which have little history to act as a guide for the future. The forecaster is left with expert opinions, market research, and historical analogies as predictive tools. High-tech companies frequently use qualitative projection techniques.

The Klabin forecast assumptions relied heavily on the causal methodology, linking Klabin's sales to GDP changes. Time series techniques assisted me in developing the relationships between product demand, GDP growth, and paper prices.

- *Macroeconomy.* The Brazilian economic recovery fosters steady growth through 2003. In 2004 and 2005 a recession cuts GDP increases to 1 percent and 3 percent, respectively.
- *Devaluation.* A 20 percent devaluation occurs in 2004. Real/US$ exchange rates decline moderately the years prior to the devaluation.
- *Sales.* The percentage increases in the Company's revenues outpace GDP growth, due to three factors: (1) presumed Brazilian and U.S. inflation averaging 6 percent and 3 percent annually, respectively, over the projected period; (2) modest real price increases in the Company's export products, resulting from higher global demand due to Asian economic recoveries; and (3) Brazilian paper and packaging demand exceeding GDP growth during the start of cycle.
- *Profit.* Margins increase substantially as a result of (1) real price increases for Klabin's products; and (2) operating leverage enjoyed from higher capacity utilization.
- *Financial expenses/income.* Local borrowings have real interest rates (i.e., exceeding inflation) of 6 percent. U.S. dollar borrowings average 11 percent annual interest. Financial income on the Company's investment portfolio yields 1 percent below interest costs.
- *Balance sheet items.* The relationships of balance sheet items to annual sales, total assets, and stockholders' equity remain consistent with prior years.

Projected Sales

Emerging market firms initially project results in local currency. Western investors—and the local managers—then convert the local

TABLE 8.4 Converting Klabin Sales Forecasts in Brazilian Reals to U.S. Dollars (in Millions)

| | Actual | Estimated | | | Forecast | | |
	1999	2000	2001	2002	2003	2004	2005
					20% Devaluation		
Net sales in reals	Rs. 1,481	Rs. 1,789	Rs. 2,081	Rs. 2,411	Rs. 2,739	Rs. 3,074	Rs. 2,292
Real/US$ exchange rate	1.82	1.86	1.90	1.96	2.02	2.52	2.57
US$ equivalent net sales	$814	$962	$1,095	$1,230	$1,356	$1,220	$1,281
US$ sales trend	—	Up	Up	Up	Up	Down	Up

Note: The 20 percent devaluation occurs in 2004.

currency forecasts into U.S. dollars—which bankers jokingly refer to as "real money."

Assuming the local currency sales forecasts are complete, the Western analyst projects the exchange rates that are used to effect the US$ conversions. In most of my transactions, Western investors selected an annual devaluation rate of between 3 percent and 5 percent for the local currency (against the US$).

In Klabin's case, the country just underwent a major devaluation. As a result, the devaluation rate is only 2 percent in the first two years, rising to 3 percent before the 20 percent decline in 2004. The U.S. dollar-equivalent calculations appear in Table 8.4.

Summary financial forecasts appear in Table 8.5. Note how US$ equivalent revenues increase steadily until the devaluation in 2004. Profit margins rise as the Company realizes operating leverage from higher utilization rates and, at the same time, it sells into a better pricing environment.

DISCOUNTED CASH FLOW VALUATION

The critical components of Klabin's DCF valuation are (1) cash dividend forecast, (2) discount rate, and (3) terminal value. The dividend projections are available from Table 8.5. The discount rate assumes a 17.5 percent rate of return requirement. Most Western investors place Brazil in the emerging market "low risk" category; and, therefore, they hope to achieve equity IRRs of 15 percent to 20 percent (see Table 6.7). By way of reference, in June 2000 the Brazil (U.S. dollar) sovereign bond due 2008 yielded 12.30 percent per annum, a 6 percent premium to U.S. Treasuries (6.30% yield). Klabin's U.S. dollar bond due 2004 yielded 11.60 percent.

The third variable—the terminal value—is problematic. Projections become less accurate as the time period lengthens, and our dividend discount model requires an ADR price prediction in 2005, five years after the purchase date. In Klabin's case, most practitioners

TABLE 8.5 Klabin Condensed Forecast Financial Data (in Millions of US$ Equivalents, Except per Share)

Income Statement	Actual 1999	Estimated 2000	Estimated 2001	Estimated 2002	Forecast 2003	Forecast 2004	Forecast 2005
					—Recession—		
Net Sales	$814	$962	$1,095	$1,230	$1,356	$1,220	$1,281
EBITDA	251	302	361	418	386	315	366
Operating profit	171	217	270	313	281	221	235
Net income	(64)	93	137	173	148	(91)	102
Earnings per ADR	(0.87)	1.26	1.85	2.36	2.01	(1.23)	1.39
Dividends per ADR	0.15	0.25	0.37	0.47	0.40	0.20	0.30
Earnings trend	—	Up	Up	Up	Down	Down	Up
Balance Sheet							
Cash	$157	$192	$227	$231	$191	$162	$163
Fixed assets	1,135	1,246	1,302	1,342	1,388	1,326	1,162
Total assets	1,783	1,984	2,093	2,156	2,181	1,980	1,987
Total debt	912	872	837	802	765	730	743
Stockholders' equity	568	647	757	895	1,013	837	916

Note: The 20 percent devaluation occurs in 2004. Despite the volatility, Klabin's results have an upward trend.

figure a terminal value by applying the historical "downcycle" P/E multiple (or EV/EBITDA multiple) to the Company's 2005 results (see Figure 8.1). An examination of Latin American paper and packaging stocks over a 10-year period suggests the following average valuation ratios:

Country Economic Performance	P/E	EV/EBITDA
Peak	6×	3.0×
Mid-cycle	10×	4.5×
Down	18×	7.5×

Note: EV/EBITDA = Enterprise value/earnings before interest, taxes, depreciation, and amortization.

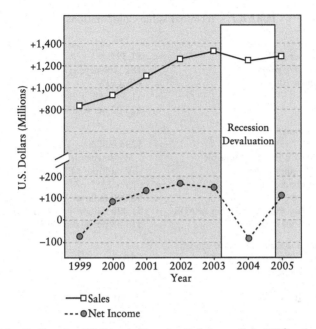

FIGURE 8.1 Industrias Klabin de Papel e Celulose, S.A. US$ sales and net income projections.

A small minority of analysts utilize the "constant growth" dividend discount model to set a terminal value. Tables 8.6 and 8.7 illustrate the P/E multiple, EV/EBITDA multiple, and DDM methods. Note that the terminal value estimates are $25, $16, and $5, respectively.

TABLE 8.6 Klabin's Share Value with a P/E-Based Terminal Value—DCF Approach

$$\text{Klabin 2000 ADR value} = \frac{D_1}{1+k} + \frac{D_2}{(1+k)^2} + \frac{D_3}{(1+k)^3} + \frac{D_5 + \text{Terminal Value}}{(1+k)^5}$$

$$= \frac{0.37}{1.175} + \frac{0.47}{1.381} + \frac{0.40}{1.622} + \frac{0.20}{1.906} + \frac{0.30 + 25.02}{2.24}$$

$$= \$12.31$$

TABLE 8.7   Terminal Value Computations

P/E Approach

2005 earnings per ADR	=	$1.39
Estimated 2005 P/E multiple	=	18x (downcycle)
Terminal value in 2005	=	P/E × EPS
	=	$1.39 × 18
	=	$25.02 per Klabin ADR

EV/EBITDA Approach

2005 EBITDA	=	$235 million
Estimated 2005 EV/EBITDA multiple	=	7.5x (downcycle)
Calculate total equity value	=	(EV multiple × EBITDA) – Klabin's Debt
Insert appropriate data	=	(7.5 × 235) – 743
Total equity value	=	$1,020 million
Divide total equity value by number of ADR	=	$1,020 million ÷ 73.8 million shares
Terminal value (2005) per ADR	=	$13.83 per Klabin ADR

Constant Growth Dividend Discount Model

2005 dividend average over 5 years[a]	=	$0.35
Constant growth rate	=	8%
Discount rate[b]	=	15%
Terminal value 2005	=	$\dfrac{D2005}{k-g}$
	=	$\dfrac{\$0.35}{.15-.08}$
	=	$5.00 per ADR

Note: I recommend using all three forms of terminal value calculation.

[a] Use 5-year average for a cyclical stock in the constant growth model.

[b] Assume Brazil is less risky by 2005. Reduce long-term discount rate to 15 percent from 17.5 percent in the constant growth model.

With these figures in hand, the rest of the DCF exercise consists of filling in the variables of the two-step dividend discount model, reviewed in Chapter 1 and covered in numerous textbooks. In the P/E-based computation, I inserted the $25 estimate of the terminal value and produced an ADR price of $12.31.

The EV/EBITDA and constant growth DDM produce current ADR prices of $7.31 and $3.37, respectively, after discounting at 17.5 percent. See Table 8.7 for terminal value comparisons.

As set forth in Figure 8.2, Klabin's ADR price at the time of this writing was $9.58. This price was reasonably close to two of the DCF appraisals (i.e., the P/E [$12.31 value] and EBITDA [$7.31 value] methods). The Constant Growth model suggested a conservative $3.37 estimate. At only 38 percent of book value, this valuation was an unrealistic outlyer and I disregarded its impact. Klabin's equity—at $9.58 per ADR—was priced reasonably close to its intrinsic value, but a buy or sell decision was elusive, since the two methodologies produced results on opposite sides of the market price.

RELATIVE VALUE APPROACH

The reliance of the DCF school on uncertain projections and arguable discount rates reduces its relevance in the real world. Indeed, Morgan Stanley analyst, Madhav Dar, suggests there is no such thing

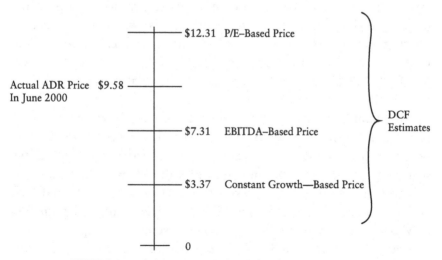

FIGURE 8.2 Klabin's ADR price versus DCF estimates.

as the intrinsic value of a stock, "You have to figure out where you are relative to everybody else," he says, "It's an investment decision overlaid by game theory." With most institutions sharing this view, practitioners turn to relative value techniques to price companies. The positive and negative aspects of a stock are evaluated against those characteristics of similar stocks falling into the same industry category, and valuation multiples become the yardsticks for comparative pricing.

As one illustration, consider the remarks of Jay Bhutani, security analyst at Donaldson Lufkin Jenrette, "One of the major factors underlying our recommendation is PKN's (a Polish refining company) attractive valuation. We believe the company is attractively valued on a cash multiple basis to its central European peers . . . On an EV/EBITDA and Price/Cash Flow basis, PKN is trading around 3.0 times, which is at a discount to other central European peers such as MOL (Hungary), OMV (Austria), and Hellenic Petroleum (Greece)."

Relative value multiples rely heavily on historical financial results, such as earnings growth and balance sheet leverage. Firms with the best historical results are usually rewarded with the highest multiples. The big problem with this approach is that share prices are eventually determined by future performance, rather than past history, so relying totally on relative valuation is like "driving a car by looking in the rear view mirror." Another problem is that many firms, particularly in the emerging markets, lack true comparables. See Table 8.8 for a summary critique of the relative value and DCF techniques.

In Klabin's case, we faced a shortage of true Brazilian comparables. Celulose Aracruz, for example, is strictly a pulp exporter, while Votorantim only manufactures paper. To broaden the sample, we searched for other Latin companies and found two Mexican firms that were active in packaging like Klabin. They were Kimberly-Clark de Mexico and Grupo Durango. The macroeconomic environments of Mexico and Brazil are different, so we essentially compared apples to oranges (see Table 8.3). Table 8.9 provides summary valuation data for the sample firms.

TABLE 8.8 Problems with Valuation Approaches

Intrinsic Value (Discounted Cash Flow)
■ Theoretically appropriate, but practitioners are reluctant to utilize discounted cash flow.
■ Difficult to reach consensus on growth and discount rate assumptions.
■ Projections are uncertain.

Relative Value
■ There is no yardstick to indicate whether the entire group of comparables is properly valued, on a commonsense basis.
■ In the emerging markets, most firms lack true comparables, diminishing the technique's relevance.
■ Relative value is overly reliant on past history, at the expense of future prospects.

TABLE 8.9 Summary Valuation Data of Latin American Packaging, Pulp, and Paper Firms (at June 2000)

Company	Country	Market Value ($MM)	Price/ Book Value	P/E	EV/ EBITDA	Financial Performance Ranking
Aracruz	Brazil	$1,970	1.1	11.6	4.3	Better
Bahia Sul	Brazil	572	0.7	5.6	4.7	Better
Grupo Durango	Mexico	243	0.5	4.3	5.4	Worse
K-C de Mexico	Mexico	3,571	2.3	11.2	5.8	Better
Klabin	Brazil	616	1.0	5.0	3.8	—
Suzano	Brazil	551	0.7	nm.	4.1	Worse
Votorantim	Brazil	1,439	1.2	6.3	4.0	Better

Note: Market value equals shares outstanding times share price (expressed in U.S. dollars).

P/E and EV/EBITDA ratios based on 2000 estimated results.

Financial performance ranking represents a combination of growth, activity, credit, and profitability ratios, all derived from historical records. Klabin is the benchmark.

A shortage of comparables forces the emerging market analyst to make comparisons across borders.

TABLE 8.10 Comparing Relative Valuations and Performance

	Price/ Book Value	P/E	EV/ EBITDA
Better Performance			
Aracruz	1.1	11.6	4.3
Bahia Sul	0.7	5.6	4.7
K-C de Mexico	2.3	11.2	5.8
Votorantim	1.2	6.3	4.0
Average of better performers	1.3	8.7	4.7
Klabin	1.0	5.0	3.8
Worse Performance			
Grupo Durango	0.5	4.3	5.4
Suzano	1.2	6.3	4.0
Average of worst performers	0.8	5.3	4.7

Note: Despite better performance, Klabin showed P/E and EV/EBITDA multiples that were slightly lower than those of Grupo Durango or Suzano. This suggested Klabin's stock was mildly undervalued.

As shown in Table 8.10, the market generally rewarded better performance with higher multiples, and no strong distinction was made between Mexican and Brazilian firms. Klabin's P/E and EBITDA ratios were slightly below the two firms that it outperformed, but its price/book value ratio was slightly higher. The difference suggested that Klabin was mildly undervalued on a relative basis.

INVESTMENT RECOMMENDATION AND SUMMARY

In this chapter, we appraised Klabin's shares and found the Company's ADR price was reasonably close to the valuation models. Unfortunately, the results were inconclusive regarding a buy or sell decision. The DCF approach produced one value 28 percent higher

FIGURE 8.3 Investors must balance the intrinsic and relative value approaches when evaluating a common stock.

than the market and one value 24 percent lower. The relative value method hinted at a buy recommendation, but it was not convincing.

In this instance, my conclusion didn't mean that Klabin was a poor stock selection. Rather, it suggested that a shareholder couldn't reasonably expect to receive a superior return. For those investors who wanted premium performance in Brazil, the Klabin analysis told them to look elsewhere.

CHAPTER 9

Commercial Lending and Fixed Income Investment in the Emerging Markets

The previous chapters covered equity portfolio investment and foreign direct investment. This chapter reviews lending hard currency to emerging market corporations. Such lending usually takes the form of a syndicated bank loan, an institutional private placement, or a public bond issue.

EMERGING MARKETS AND FOREIGN LENDERS

To begin, the emerging markets have not been kind to foreign lenders. Over the last 25 years, more than 60 emerging market governments defaulted on foreign currency bond and bank debt. The sovereign defaults usually led to massive private sector defaults. Recessions triggered by the defaults and accompanying devaluations hurt corporate earnings, which put pressure on the corporations' ability to service debt. Typically, the government instituted tight exchange controls to reserve hard currency for essential imports like food, energy, and medicine. This latter action made foreign currency scarce or, at times, completely unavailable, for those local companies that needed to pay foreign debt service. When Brazil defaulted in the early 1980s, for example, Unibanco, a leading bank, made millions from operations, but it couldn't access the dollars to pay its U.S. lenders.

Of the top 12 emerging markets listed in Chapter 1, seven defaulted on their sovereign obligations during the last 25 years, and it is highly likely that two others, Korea and Thailand, would have defaulted in the 1997 meltdown, if not for the huge bailouts provided to them by the IMF. Despite the spotty track record, 5 of the 12 sovereigns enjoyed "foreign currency" investment grade ratings from Standard & Poor's Corporation at December 2000, suggesting their debt was as risky as the debt of Marriott or Lockheed Martin in the United States.

Given the many risks of the emerging markets, I was always surprised at the large number of Western institutions willing to loan money there. The commercial banks I knew said that ancillary financial services boosted their loan returns, but the foreign pension funds, mutual funds, and insurance companies had no such excuse. They routinely risked $1,000 of principal in a Malaysian conglomerate, for example, to gain an 8 percent yield, rather than depositing the proceeds with a relatively safe U.S. firm at a 6 percent yield. For the extra $20 per year, the Western institution bore substantial political, currency and information risk, all of what threatened the prospects of keeping the $1,000 intact.

Multiply that institution by the thousands, and imagine their panic during the 1997 Asian crisis, when they faced substantial losses on their emerging market loan and bond investments. You can then understand why the IMF, World Bank, and G-7 nations engineered sovereign bailouts totaling tens of billions of dollars. Western institutions applied tremendous pressure on these organizations to provide the relief, which enabled their Third World investments to stay reasonably intact. Otherwise, the resultant losses could have sparked a financial calamity, as these large investors would have deserted risky investments en masse for the safe haven of blue chip stocks and bonds.

Of course the investment environment is not always dicey, and many experienced hands play against the grain. A sophisticated technique is to buy emerging market corporate bonds immediately after a crisis. Established local firms will have issued bonds that then trade for a fraction of par value, presenting yields-to-maturity of 25 percent or 30 percent. When the country's finances stabilize, bond prices can easily double, as these yields approach normal levels of 12 percent to 13 percent.

LENDERS VERSUS EQUITY INVESTORS

The concerns of a long-term lender—whether the borrower is located in an emerging market or not—are different than those of an equity investor. The lender's expected rate-of-return is fixed, and it does not get paid a substantially greater yield for taking on a speculative risk. As a result, its foremost objective is maintaining safety of principal (i.e., getting paid back 100 cents on the dollar), while achieving its risk-adjusted return. The equity investor, in contrast, has an unlimited upside when a company is successful, and for that reason, it is willing to assume more risk and accept a higher loss rate than a lender.

Lenders are more circumspect than equity investors about losing money. In part, this risk aversion relates to the nature of the lending business. Pension funds and insurance companies essentially run "matched books" whereby the future cash flows from long-term assets, like loans and bonds, are paired with the forecast liabilities owed to retirees and claimants. These firms can ill-afford defaulted loans that upset the matching process. Commercial banks and finance companies operate similar matching programs of assets and liabilities, but they function with higher degrees of leverage, as much as 12 to 1 in the case of a commercial bank. With such a small equity base, a bank cannot afford to take a major loss on speculative loans. Should creditors see the bank's equity base shrink, the bank's ability to roll over its own obligations would be in question.

CREDIT ANALYSIS PROCESS

To quantify risk and pricing, Western institutions that lend to emerging market firms use credit analysis, which is the research process undertaken by a lender prior to making the decision to lend. During credit analysis, the lender assesses the strengths and weaknesses associated with the borrower, the risks involved with the loan, and the likelihood of repayment.

In the book, *Credit Analysis* (New York: John Wiley & Sons, 1983), Roger Hale summarizes the foundation of credit analysis:

> *The fundamentals of modern credit analysis are twofold: First is the examination of the nature of the borrower's business in the context of its industry, and second is the analysis of cash flow. The purpose of the former is to understand the comparative market position of the firm, the pressures of competition, the risk and reward structure of the industry, the barriers to entry, the degree of technological change, and so on. The purpose of cash flow analysis, on the other hand, is to disentangle from financial statements based on historical accounting principles the actual movements of cash in terms of its sources and uses. Once these past sources and uses have been examined, a reasonable estimate can be made as the future sources and uses, and this can be combined with the understanding of the borrower already gained to permit a judgement to be made as to the borrower's credit worthiness.*

Hale notes that credit analysis looks at both the borrower's business and its cash flow position. This goes well beyond the simple calculation of historical financial ratios and the rudimentary extrapolation of past results into the future. Lenders must gain an understanding of the underlying business, industry and economic environment, as well as a knowledge of the borrower's likely financial performance.

The Westerner's evaluation of an emerging market company's borrowing capability follows the methodical process outlined by Mr. Hale, with a few additions. Initially, the foreign lender judges the borrower's ability to repay local currency-denominated obligations. After all, if it can't pay home country banks, how will it send hard currency to foreigners? This basic screen takes the form of a top-down study (outlined in Chapter 7), which provides the basis for financial projections (as illustrated in the Klabin case in Chapter 8). By preparing multiple scenarios under differing competitive and macroeconomic environments, the lender assesses the borrower's prospective ability to repay a loan. Of particular interest to a lender is the borrower's creditworthiness under a worst case analysis, since the lender gets paid the same interest rate in good or bad times. See Table 9.1 for a review of the process.

Assuming the company passes the first screen of local creditworthiness, the next step is to determine how it fares with foreign-currency borrowings. If they haven't already, most Western lenders then convert the borrower's local currency forecasts into U.S. dollars, using expected future exchange rates. In Chapter 8, we completed this task with Klabin. (See Table 9.2 for Klabin's forecast credit ratios.) To these U.S. dollar projections, the lender applies stress tests that are more severe than one uses in a developed country setting.

TABLE 9.1 Emerging Market Credit Analysis for the Hard Currency Lender

Step 1:	Perform top-down evaluation of the borrower's business and prepare related financial projections in local currency. Determine creditworthiness in local currency.
Step 2:	Convert all local currency forecasts into US$, using expected future exchange rates. Determine if borrower can service foreign currency obligations under various stress tests, such as deep recessions and devaluations.
Step 3:	Overlay the likelihood of the sovereign interfering with (1) foreign currency exchange, (2) the industry's economics, or (3) the borrower's specific business. Can interference disrupt the firm's ability to make money and pay US$ to its foreign lenders?
Step 4:	Consider ways in which the structure of the proposed loan, private placement or bond mitigates the sovereign risks.

TABLE 9.2 Industrias Klabin de Papel e Celulose, S.A.

	Actual	Estimated	Forecast				
	1999	2000	2001	2002	2003	2004	2005
						–Recession–	
EBIT/interest	2.0×	2.4×	3.4×	3.9×	3.5×	2.9×	3.1×
EBITDA/debt service	1.7	1.1	1.6	1.4	3.0	1.3	1.5
Total debt/equity	1.6	1.3	1.1	0.9	0.8	0.9	0.8
Total debt/total debt plus equity	0.6	0.6	0.5	0.5	0.4	0.5	0.4

Note: Excludes noncash foreign exchange losses.

FIGURE 9.1 International lenders must redouble their credit analysis in the emerging markets.

For example, in evaluating Latin American corporate loans, the International Finance Corporation (and the international banks that participated in its loan syndications) routinely incorporated downside scenarios whereby a borrower's home country underwent a 5 percent devaluation (against the US$) every year and a severe recession every five years. (We used a similar scenario in the Klabin case.) In project finance deals involving an export commodity, pessimistic assumptions were also common. Syndicate banks insisted that IFC run scenarios in which the commodity traded at a cyclical low for extended periods. If the prospective borrower covered its debt service charts under these extreme conditions by a minimum factor of 1.25×, the deal had a good chance of meeting approvals. In effect, the emerging market borrower was held to a higher credit standard—absent sovereign risk—than a similar U.S. or European firm. (See Figure 9.1.)

The only problem with this approach is that it is unrealistic. One time devaluations can approach 50 percent (against the U.S.) in a month's time, followed by a steep recession. If this scenario is programmed into the analysis, few applicants make the grade, and the lenders don't make many loans.

Bill Chambers, Managing Director of Standard & Poor's, the leading international credit rating agency, echoes this approach to emerging market credit evaluation:

Other things being constant, a borrower in a less affluent or more volatile economy—conditions that often coincide with a lower sovereign rating—must have a more robust business position (superior market position, lower cost position, and so forth) and hold a stronger financial position (higher profitability, higher interest coverage and stronger capitalization) than a similar company located in a less challenging or more favorable environment—which often corresponds to a higher sovereign rating—to achieve the same issuer credit rating. This is because of the greater uncertainty of doing business in the more difficult economic environment and the potential for greater unpredictability of financial results, among other concerns.

It is difficult to put a number on how much better the emerging market company has to be in order to receive the same credit standing as a Western borrower. Besides having a more solid market position, a longer track record, and a prominent family owner, my experience indicates that the emerging market firm needs to have pro forma leverage ratios (i.e., as if the loan was made) at least 20 percent to 25 percent better than a similar company in the developed world. If the Western firm has a debt service coverage ratio of 2.0 times, then the Third World company needs a 2.5 times ratio to obtain similar treatment. If the First World company has a debt to total capitalization ratio of 50 percent, the emerging market enterprise better have a ratio of 40 percent or less. Here, the terms *similar treatment* means access to capital; the pricing on the loan is a function of market forces in the loan and bond markets, where Third World customers pay a premium.

POLITICAL RISK AND CREDIT ANALYSIS

The third step of the analysis is gauging the degree by which political risk affects the borrower's ability to make U.S. dollar payments to offshore lenders. In the past, a common problem for international lenders has been a government imposing controls that limit a borrower's ability to change local currency into U.S. dollars. Without this hard currency, the borrower can't service its foreign debt obligations, even if it is profitable and has substantial local monies. The likelihood of this situation occurring is called *transfer risk*. History shows that transfer risk is highest when a sovereign experiences its own macroeconomic difficulties, and foreign exchange is viewed as a scarce and valuable commodity.

The principal credit rating agencies, Standard & Poor's and Moody's Investor Services, equate a country's transfer risk with the credit rating of the sovereign's U.S. dollar denominated bonds. The lower the bond rating, the higher the likelihood of a transfer problem. Since the sovereign has the unilateral power to impose foreign exchange controls over private borrowers, the rating agency view gives rise to the notion of a "sovereign ceiling," whereby local borrowers with hard currency loans can never achieve a U.S. dollar credit rating higher than the government. (See Table 9.3 for selected sovereign debt ratings.) Exceptions to this rule are specially designed transactions that limit the sovereign's ability to interfere with debt service. This topic is covered later in the chapter.

Besides transfer risk, the foreign lender is exposed to the panoply of political risks discussed in Chapter 6. Depending on the severity of the government action (or inaction), a borrower's earnings power and debt service capability are vulnerable. For example, if the Indonesian government dropped the 65 percent duty on imports of processed marble, the profit margin of PT Citatah, a prominent local marble miner and processor, would be damaged. Its principal lender, a Japanese bank consortium, would see the recovery potential of its loan reduced. Likewise, if the Karachi Electric Supply Company, a Pakistani

TABLE 9.3 Sovereign Long-Term Credit Ratings for Foreign Currency Debt (December 2000)

Principal Emerging Markets	S&P Credit Rating
	Investment Grade
Poland	BBB+
China	BBB
South Korea	BBB
South Africa	BBB–
Thailand	BBB–
	Junk Bond Status
Mexico	BB+
Argentina	BB
India	BB
Brazil	B+
Turkey	B+
Indonesia	In default
Russia	In default

government company, abrogated its 22-year obligation to buy electricity from Tapal Energy Limited, a generating firm owned by Wartsila Diesel (Sweden), Marubeni (Japan), and Ameejee Valleejee (Pakistan), then Tapal's foreign lenders would see their loan values significantly diminish. Political actions can have the opposite of weakening creditworthiness. For example, in the late 1990s, Argentina gave away valuable telecommunications spectrum to connected groups, thus boosting their capacity to generate cash by selling the related licenses.

MITIGATING POLITICAL RISK

In a small percentage of transactions, borrower and lender work to structure a deal that substantially reduces the possibility of a government action disrupting the US$ flow to the lender. In most cases, these transactions involve the borrower securitizing—for the lender's benefit—either (1) a revolving pool of offshore U.S. dollar–dominated assets; or (2) a future stream of U.S. dollar-denominated revenues from export sales. The offshore nature of the related assets and revenues limits the legal ability of the sovereign in seizing the foreign exchange. In a smaller number of deals, the parties involve multilateral lending institutions like the World Bank or its private-sector affiliate, the IFC.

The multilaterals, which lend in U.S. dollars like international banks, generally enjoy a preferred status relative to private lenders. When emerging market governments default on U.S. dollar commercial bank loans and public bonds, they almost always reserve enough hard cash to keep the IMF, World Bank, and multilateral creditors current. The same goes for corporate loan syndicates led by the IFC or the Inter-American Development Bank. Almost always, these obligations are exempted from foreign exchange controls, and their susceptibility to other political risks is historically very low. As a result, lenders assign a higher degree of creditworthiness to these deals in comparison to a transaction without multilateral involvement.

Long referred to as a "halo effect" in the international banking community, the value of the multilateral association was quantified by a landmark transaction that I pioneered while working at the IFC. In 1995, an $85 million IFC-syndicated loan for Apasco, S.A., a Mexican cement company, broke through the sovereign ceiling by receiving a BBB+ rating. At the time, the Mexican sovereign was rated BB+, and Apasco's local bonds were rated BB+. The novel structure saved Apasco over $1 million annually in interest costs, and the investment-grade rating enabled it to obtain a 12-year tenor, when other prominent firms settled for 3-year maturities.

TOP-DOWN ANALYSIS AND CREDIT EVALUATION

The top-down analysis involved in constructing a good credit evaluation is similar to the process involved in appraising an equity investment. The lender studies the borrower's country, the related macroeconomic forecast, the relevant industry concerns and various company-specific matters. The end result is a series of financial projections that indicate whether the prospective borrower can repay the loan in a timely fashion.

As noted earlier, the lender's return is fixed. It has no significant upside if the borrower's earnings double or triple, but it suffers major losses in principal value should the company default or restructure its obligations in hard times. As a result, the U.S. dollar lender, particularly in the emerging markets, is generally more circumspect than it is in its home country. The following outline reviews the borrower characteristics favored by international lenders.

Emerging Market Companies and US$ Borrowings Attributes Favored by International Lenders

Financial Attributes

- *Growing sales and operating income.* The company should be showing steady progress.

- *Explainable volatility.* Sharp changes in financial performance should be explained by recessions or devaluations, rather than competition or product obsolescence.
- *Size.* Western institutions rarely extend long-term loans of under $10 million in the emerging markets. Small deals are uneconomical, due to the costs of investigation, documentation, and maintenance. Since most lenders want to represent less than one-half of debt outstanding, the company's effective capitalization (including equity) should therefore be at least $40 million, making it a significant enterprise in many emerging markets. Lenders prefer large borrowers for another reason. Prominent firms are more likely to adhere to rules of conduct followed by Western borrowers.
- *Low debt to equity ratio.* Debt to capitalization (for an industrial company) should be no more than 40 percent to 50 percent. This allows a financial cushion if a substantial recession occurs.
- *Hard assets.* The left side of the balance sheet should be comprised of hard assets, like accounts receivable, inventory, and fixed plant. This gives the lender something to mortgage, which is important. A secured lender has a strong position in any debt restructuring. Hard assets are critical for two other reasons. (1) goodwill is tough to appraise in the Third World, and (2) cash flow lending has not caught on with local banks.
- *Debt service coverage.* Available cash flows should cover estimated debt service by 1.5 times at a minimum. Devaluation stress tests should show coverage of at least 1.1 times. To cover lump-sum bond maturities, the forecast uses averaging.
- *Debt maturities.* The company's debt maturities should ideally be staggered, so that a major portion of debt does not mature in any one year. The key risk is that the country has a macroeconomic problem in that one year; and, as a result, the company cannot refinance its obligations, forcing it to default.
- *US$ revenues.* A portion of the firm's business should relate to the export market. This brings in hard currency for loan repayment and demonstrates international competitiveness.

■ *Cross guaranties.* The lender should verify that the borrower has limited direct and indirect guaranties of third-party indebtedness.

The Borrower's Business

■ *Oligopoly.* The preferred borrower is a member of an oligopoly that maintains price discipline. Since most emerging markets are small, an internationally competitive player is likely to be so big as to have a leading market share.

■ *Low customer concentration.* Most borrower businesses emphasize the home market. This concentration problem shouldn't be compounded by the firm having a few big customers.

■ *Manufacturer.* As cited earlier, the service and intellectual property industries are not the focus of large Third World businesses. Manufacturers remain the preferred borrowers.

■ *Low-technology.* In both emerging and developed markets, lenders prefer low-tech firms where the pace of product change is slow and earnings are reasonably predictable.

■ *Scale.* The company's product line should conform to its market. A borrower shouldn't be making refrigerators in Costa Rica, for example. The local market is too small to make refrigerator production a viable enterprise. Only the export platform of a multinational is appropriate for that type of manufacture.

■ *Natural resource business.* Emerging market firms that extract and process natural resources are attractive, particularly if they export a portion of their production. Optimally, a portion of future sales should be hedged to reduce price volatility.

■ *Product pricing and costing.* The business should make a familiar product, the pricing and costing of which can be compared easily to a similar item in the developed world. Comparative analysis enables the lender to determine if the company (1) can withstand foreign entrants to the local market; and (2) has the potential to export and compete with international players.

■ *Brand names.* An established brand name is an entry barrier that lenders like.

- *Import quotas, tariffs, domestic regulations.* These government-based factors protect the borrower from foreign competition; however, if these protections were reduced, the company would still prosper, albeit at a lower level of profitability.
- *Strong alliances.* The borrower should be affiliated with the appropriate elite family in its home country. An alliance with a large multinational is also evidence of creditworthiness.
- *Professional management.* The lender prefers a company that recruits professional managers as well as family members.

The Deal's Structure

- *Secured loan.* In the emerging markets, a secured lender is in a far stronger position—vis-à-vis unsecured lenders—than it is in a Western setting. In the past, certain borrowers have discriminated against foreign unsecured lenders by selling assets and paying local creditors first with the proceeds. In a June 1999 ruling, the Supreme Court indicated that U.S. unsecured creditors must go to local jurisdictions for relief from such actions, even when their note agreement is under U.S. law. Thus, a mortgage on fixed assets is highly desirable, since they can't be sold without the lender collecting the proceeds.
- *Subsidiary guarantee.* When loaning to a holding company that houses its operations in several subsidiaries, the foreign lender is well-advised to have the operating companies guarantee the parent's loan. This action presents subsidiary creditors from exercising seniority rights and it strengthens the lender's hand in a restructuring.
- *Restrictive covenants.* Lenders and bondholders should fight to obtain meaningful restrictions on the borrower's conduct in their legal agreements. For example, before paying large dividends, incurring sizeable debts or making investments outside of its industry, the borrower should consult first with its lenders. Many emerging market bond issues have minimal covenants, and lenders thus give management too free a hand.

■ *Prestigious bank lead.* Bank loan syndicates led by prestigious institutions, like Chase, are perceived to carry less risk than a syndicate led by smaller banks, such as Comerica Bank, or Bank of Boston. If payment problems arise, Chase carries a bigger stick with the local business and government communities.

■ *Offshore assets/preferred creditor involvement.* Export receivable securitization and multilateral syndication reduced sovereign risk and enhance a borrower's creditworthiness.

When Western commercial banks and bond underwriters apply the above attributes to emerging market firms, they quickly discover that only a handful meet the tests. During good times, the competition among foreign lenders for these few companies is intense. In 1995, for example, when the Thai economy was running on eight cylinders, Japanese banks threw money at blue-chip Thai companies, offering seven-year U.S. dollar loans at LIBOR plus 90 basis points. Similar operations in the United States paid the same rate, despite a much safer macroenvironment.

The old saying that "bankers will offer you an umbrella when the sun shines, but not when it rains" applies to the developing economies. In times of crisis, foreign money dries up, as no lender wants to gauge the timing and breadth of recovery. By way of illustration, in March 1995 I managed a $57 million financing for Sigma Alimentos, S.A., the Mexican food processor. The deal was the first syndicated loan to close after the December 1994 devaluation, which had put Mexico into a serious recession. Convincing U.S. and European banks to participate in the deal required voluminous due diligence on my part, as their credit officers were skeptical of any turnaround forecast.

INTEREST RATES

The principal attraction of the emerging markets to Western lenders is the high interest rate environment. For U.S. dollar loans, Third

World borrowers routinely pay 1½ percent to 3 percent more than comparably-rated U.S. companies. Thus, when Merrill Lynch & Co. marketed a 10-year structured financing for TGN (Argentina), the interest rate was 4⅞ percent over the U.S. Treasury. At the same time, equally-rated U.S. industrials (BBB- rating) were paying 2½ percent over Treasuries, 2⅜ percent less than TGN. Similarly, the B-rated bonds of Globo Cabo, the Brazilian cable-television firm, traded at 13 percent in July 2000. The B-rated bonds of U.S. communication firms (Chancellor, Charter, and Williams) yielded an average of 10 percent, or 3 percent lower. Explaining the divergence, AIG portfolio executive, Jerry Herman, said, "The bond ratings only explain so much. Political, currency, and transfer risk judgments are highly subjective; and, furthermore, in any troubled situation, the foreign lender stands on uncertain ground from a legal point of view, relative to a U.S. bond deal. These factors contribute to the premium yields."

While Third World borrowers always paid a premium, the spreads base have widened since the 1997 Asian crisis. "Banks and bond investors have retrenched," says Stefania Berla, a loan syndications manager. "The 'cold-nose' buyers—the investors that wanted to diversify and get yield—have disappeared from the emerging markets. 1997 made them wake up to the currency risk." The fewer number of buyers inevitably mean high interest rates for Third World companies. Furthermore, other high-yield alternatives—without currency risk—provide a viable alternative for investors. The European junk bond market, for example, has multiplied in size several times over the last few years. European leveraged buyouts carry low credit ratings, but they avoid the political risk and currency problems.

A few participants believe this is a short-term phenomenon. Acknowledging the recent trend, Laura Feinland-Katz, Managing Director at Standard & Poor's, says, "The emerging markets hit a rough patch, but it's a matter of time before the U.S. high-yield investors come back in. Most investors have short memories. They're not out of this market for good." Her words ring true. When the Russian government and many companies defaulted on their debts in 1998, Western lenders warned that the country would be frozen out of capital markets for years, but high interest rates and up-front fees have a way of erasing bad memories. In August 2000, OAO Yukos, a Russian oil company, closed a $50 million syndicated loan for nine months at 3.25 percent over LIBOR. Ironically, after the 1998 crash, Yukos went out of its way to stiff foreign creditors. An affiliate of the company, Bank Menatep, defaulted on a $236 million loan from Western lenders that was backed by 30 percent of Yukos stock. When the banks collected their collateral, the company effected a series of share dilutions and asset dispositions that made the collateral nearly worthless. Eventually, the lenders sold the shares back to Yukos at a big loss.

Two additional factors contribute to a yield premium. The smaller group of buyers and sellers—relative to U.S. corporate bonds—limits the liquidity for emerging market paper, and investors want extra yield for this marketability shortcoming. And many institutions place artificial allocation restrictions on the emerging market asset class, thereby limiting demand and pushing up yields.

These 1½ percent to 3 percent premiums may seem egregious to U.S. borrowers, but the local alternatives for emerging market firms are frequently worse (see Table 9.4). The interest rates in developing nations are onerous by Western standards for they often exceed inflation by 10 percent or more. For example, 1999 inflation in the Dominican Republic was only 5 percent, yet local banks were charging prime borrowers a 24 percent interest rate and offering a maximum maturity of a mere nine months. Tricom, S.A. a local telecommunications firm with US$22 million in annual profit, successfully sought economical U.S. dollar loans. Even with the Dominican Republic's dismal B+ sovereign ceiling, the firm secured intermediate-loans in the U.S. markets at 10 percent to 12 percent. Assuming no radical devaluation, going abroad provided substantial savings to the company, and fewer refinancing risks (see Table 9.5).

TABLE 9.4 Why Do Emerging Market Firms Pay Higher Interest Rates Than U.S. Firms with the Same Credit Rating?

▣ Subjective rating criteria	Political risk, currency devaluation risk and transfer risk are difficult to quantify, even for the rating agencies. Western investors want something extra for the judgement calls.
▣ Frequent imbalance between supply and demand	Many institutional investors place strict limits on emerging market exposure. Commercial banks focus on local blue-chip firms in allocating loan volume. The limited supply vs. demand drives up rates, particularly after the 1997 crises.
▣ 1997 crisis spooked investors	The 1997 Asian crisis alerted lenders to the risks. The knee-jerk reaction was to back away from the sector.
▣ Illiquidity	The greater degree of illiquidity (vs. U.S. bonds) for Third World issues requires a yield premium.

STRUCTURED FINANCINGS AND PREFERRED CREDITOR STATUS

As stated earlier, foreign loans made directly to emerging market companies expose lenders to sovereign and currency risks. At the same time, these deals stick borrowers with high interest costs and short maturities. To avoid some of these problems, many borrowers seek structured financings or multilateral-assisted deals. The special nature of these transactions enable the borrower to break through the "sovereign ceiling," gain an investment-grade debt rating, and obtain favorable terms.

These protections offered by these transactions are real. Suzanne Abers of the International Structured Finance Group of Fitch IBCA, Duff & Phelps reports, "Of the 120 structured deals that we've rated, there have been no defaults. The performance of

TABLE 9.5　Emerging Markets Sovereign Yields (at June 2000)

	5-Year Yield	Spread over U.S. Treasury*
United States	6.00%	—
Investment Grade Rating		
Poland	7.65	165 b.p.
China	7.55	155
South Korea	8.25	225
South Africa	9.55	355
Thailand	8.00	200
Junk Bond Status		
Mexico	8.85%	285 b.p.
Argentina	12.50	650
Brazil	11.40	540
Turkey	10.35	435
Indonesia	13.25	725
Russia	17.40	1140

* A basis point (b.p.) is $\frac{1}{100}$th of a percentage point.
Note: The junk bond ratings of many emerging markets produce high capital costs.

these transactions has been excellent." Bear in mind this experience covers various economic crises in the developing countries over the last ten years, including currency devaluations, transfer problems, and sovereign defaults.

Structured Financings

Traditional structured financing developed in the United States securitized existing assets such as mortgages, auto loans, and credit cards. The lender effectively looks to the assets for loan repayment, rather than the company generating the assets. These transactions separate the risk of the asset originator, and so insulate the lenders from an originating company bankruptcy. If the value of the mortgage, auto loans, and credit cards declines below the value of the loan, the lender has a problem, since its recourse to the company is generally minimal. Figure 9.2 provides a diagram of a structured financing.

In the emerging markets, the borrower's securitized transaction relies on assets that do not yet exist, but will be generated in the future. This arrangement is referred to as a *future flow* transaction. Receivables generated from the future export of products (such as copper) or services (such as international phone calls) are pledged to an offshore subsidiary of the originating company. The subsidiary collects on the U.S. dollar-denominated receivables and pays the relevant U.S. dollar debt service. Surplus funds are then remitted to the home country.

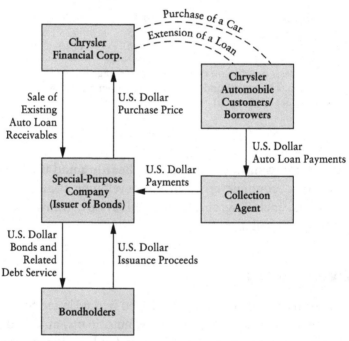

Note: In this traditional securitized financing, a package of existing loans are sold to a special-purpose company, which issues bonds to raise the purchase price.

FIGURE 9.2   Traditional securitized financing.

The future flow design has a heavy operational element. For U.S. dollar receivables to be continuously generated, the company has to provide a product or service and export it. The lender is therefore reliant on the company staying in business, which is different than a U.S.-style securitization. To reduce operational uncertainties, lenders restrict these transactions to established firms, with a solid history of exporting a commodity-type product or service.

The export customers of the company behind the future flow deal often participate in the transaction. They sign contracts that require them to send payments to the offshore accounts. Lenders make sure these customers are creditworthy enough to buy the product over the length of the loan.

Trikem Export Trust Example

In 1997, Trikem Export Trust issued $100 million, 6.73 percent investor certificates due 2004. The bonds received an A rating from Standard & Poor's, at a time when Brazil, the home country of Trikem S.A., had a BB– debt rating. The debts of the Trust were to be paid from accounts receivable generated by export sales of Trikem's products to Nissho Iwai, a Japanese trading company. Trikem manufactured commodity petrochemicals that enjoyed a broad customer base. If Nissho Iwai defaulted on its obligations under a long-term purchase contract, Trikem could have found other buyers. Figure 9.3 outlines the deal's structure.

Instituto Costarricense de Electricidad Example

In 1997, Instituto Costarricense de Electrididad (ICE), the telephone and electricity company in Costa Rica, issued $50 million of bonds due 2006. The bonds received a BBB rating at a time when the sovereign's debt was rated BB. As collateral, ICE pledged net settlement

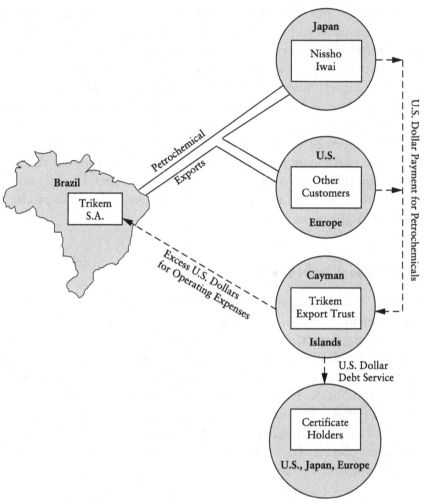

Note: US$ export revenues are kept "offshore" until foreign debt service is paid. Nissho Iwai promises to buy petrochemicals for seven years.

FIGURE 9.3 Trikem Export Trust debt financing structure.

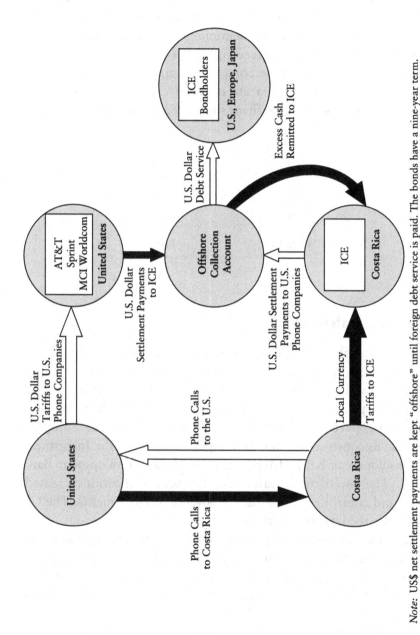

Note: US$ net settlement payments are kept "offshore" until foreign debt service is paid. The bonds have a nine-year term.

FIGURE 9.4   Instituto Costarricense de Electricidad (ICE) debt financing structure.

payments from international phone carriers, which were placed in an offshore collection account. Since incoming calls to Costa Rica historically exceeded outgoing calls by a wide margin, the lenders believed net settlement receipts, denominated in U.S. dollars, would more than cover debt service (see Figure 9.4).

Four international phone companies agreed to deposit all payments due ICE into the separate offshore collection account. The strong credit ratings of these firms supported the transaction's credit standing:

	Bond Rating
AT&T	AA–
Sprint	A–
MCI	A
World Com	BBB–

Multilateral Assistance

Although multilateral banks are known primarily for doling out loans to governments, they have arms that directly assist private investment as well. The most active of these efforts is the International Finance Corporation, an affiliate of the World Bank. Other multilaterals with departments that copy IFC's approach are the European Bank for Reconstruction and Development (EBRD), the Interamerican Development Bank (IADB), and the Asian Development Bank (ADB). The multilateral banks are financial institutions created, owned and controlled by a group of sovereign governments. The G-7 nations are the largest stockholders.

In making loans to emerging market governments, these multilaterals enjoy preferred creditor status. Even when client governments default on bonds and commercial bank loans, they allocate a portion of their scarce foreign exchange to service multilateral obligations, and the multilaterals never participate in debt reschedulings with normal commercial lenders. This exemption from transfer risk extends to private companies that borrow from IFC, EBRD, and others. Excluding this exception, the multilateral and its participating lenders are subject to normal business risks involved in any private company investment.

In a typical deal, the multilateral lends to a creditworthy emerging market company. The loan is then divided into A and B portions. The A loan is funded by the multilateral's own resources, while the B loan is sold to various banks and institutions. Since the multilateral is the lender of record, the home country sovereign treats the entire loan as a multilateral asset. (See Figure 9.5.)

The record of foreign exchange being made available to these syndicated loans is excellent, and the structure has survived numerous devaluation crises and defaults. Dependent on the multilaterals for developmental funding, Third World nations are reluctant to offend these institutions by interfering with their private sector loans. As a result, the multilateral affiliation has made the loans relatively free of expropriation and legal discrimination problems.

The multilaterals are conservative lenders. They select the most creditworthy companies and lend principally in the larger countries, where political risk is diminished. The IFC, for example, has 50 percent of its portfolio in just six countries. Furthermore, these institutions exclude industries that they don't consider developmental, such as real estate, trading, and gaming. As a result, most emerging market firms don't qualify for multilateral assistance.

DEBT FINANCING FOR NATURAL RESOURCE PROJECTS

Multinational companies that specialize in natural resources have long used project financing in the emerging markets. In a typical deal, the multinational sets up a special purpose company to exploit

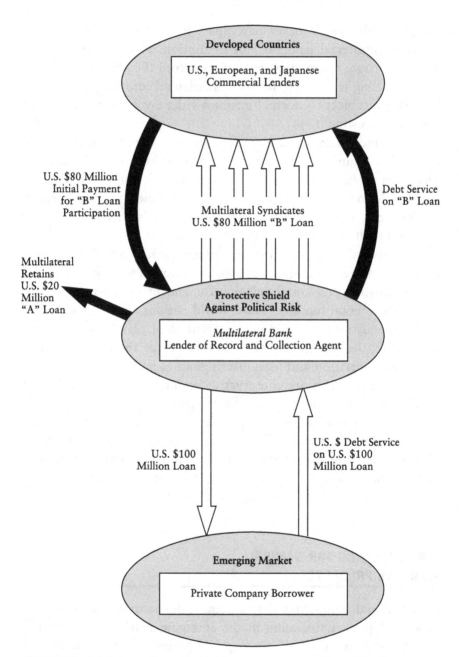

FIGURE 9.5 Multilateral syndicated loan to an emerging market borrower.

an oil field, ore body, or gas reserve. By pledging to export the natural resource for hard currency, the company raises the money to build the physical infrastructure, acquire the equipment, and hire the workforce needed to develop the resource and ship it overseas. Customers remit all sales proceeds to an offshore account, from which lenders are paid.

To support the project in its start-up phase, the multinational agrees to guarantee the company's debts for a short period of time. After the project operates successfully for 12 to 18 months, the guarantees fall away and the lenders rely solely on the company's ability to generate cash from operations. Generally, two or three multinationals join forces in promoting a project to spread the risk. (See Figure 9.6.)

SECONDARY MARKET FOR EMERGING MARKET FIXED INCOME INVESTMENTS

Up to now, we have reviewed the credit process from the point of view of the buy-and-hold lender. This framework dominates the new issue market, but when original lenders decide to sell an investment, they enter the secondary market.

The secondary market is divided into two sectors: (1) sovereign debt and (2) corporate debt. The sovereign market is the more active sector. Issue sizes are larger than corporate deals and the resultant liquidity means dealers are willing to take inventory positions. Furthermore, the information disclosure by sovereigns is considered superior to the corporate variety, enabling investors to make better trading decisions. And finally, the troubled sovereigns have found rationality in working with the finance community toward market-friendly debt resolutions. This attitude, which was demonstrated in recent debtor negotiations by Russia, Ecuador, Ukraine, and Pakistan, not only gives traders a guiding precedent, but also the confidence that they won't get blindsided.

The market for distressed corporate debt is dicier than that of the sovereigns. Besides the informational and legal problems discussed

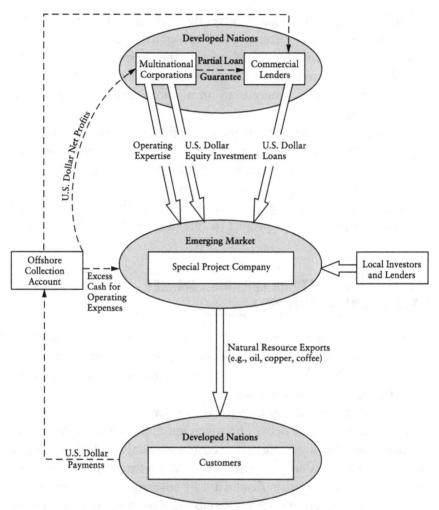

Note: Once the special project company has commenced operations, the multinationals' partial guarantee of its debts gradually disappears.

FIGURE 9.6 Typical project financing in the emerging markets.

earlier, creditors face a "lack of debt mentality," according to one Asian fund manager, "When they issued these bonds, they (the owners) had no sense that the debt had a claim on assets if it wasn't repaid." A Latin American lawyer practicing in the United States asserts a similar view, "For many Latin operators, they see a loan as a gift, rather than an obligation." Secondary investors are more direct than original lenders in confronting these attitudes. "We're not afraid to foreclose," says another fund manager, "We may have gotten in at only 25 cents on the dollar; so we've got a lot less to lose than the bank that loaned at 100 cents."

Three years after the Asian crisis, Nick Cournoyer, Managing Director of London-based Montpelier Asset Management, is optimistic over Asian restructuring efforts, "The restructuring process is unfolding better now. The second- and third-generation owners are willing to work with foreign creditors and the finance ministries are taking an active role." The key to investing in secondary paper is to select companies with a viable business and a management team that can formulate a sustainable debt load. "Owners are starting to change their tune on equity," he says, "as long as they have a buy-back option from the lenders."

The evidence indicates that distressed emerging market debt finds buyers when the price falls low enough. For example, sovereign Russian debt traded as low as 13 cents on the dollar in 1998. Ecuador's debt fell to 23 percent of par after its default in 1999, and Indonesian corporate debt in 2000 traded at 25 cents to 30 cents on the dollar. In certain cases, the people doing the buying are the owners, who withdraw money from their Singapore and Swiss bank accounts to effect the local purchases. At other times, the buyers are vulture funds and prominent institutions. Lehman Brothers and Goldman Sachs, for example, operate highly regarded distressed debt funds. A well-timed purchase can provide significant returns. The aforementioned Russian debt, for example, traded at 91 percent in August 2000, providing a 600 percent return in two years.

TEN CREDIT GUIDELINES

Before making corporate loans in the emerging markets, Western lenders should consider ten guidelines:

1. *Be mindful of the cycles.* Emerging market economies are volatile, as are the sentiments of the Western investors that pursue them. In analyzing the degree of risk in a business loan, the lender should not assume that an economy's progress will continue indefinitely into the future. The loan (or bond) should withstand theoretical devaluations and recessions. Mario Repetto, an Argentine investment banker, recalls Wall Street's fascination with Argentine credits in 1998, "When the window was open, they were all pushing to loan money here."

2. *Prominent backers are critical.* The participation of prominent multinationals, home-country business groups, and local families are critical in the success of an emerging market company. Ensure that the borrower has one or more of these players before proceeding.

3. *Understand the business.* The operating and financial analysis of an emerging market company is usually more involved than its Western counterpart. As a lender, be prepared to do " private equity style" due diligence before making a commitment. Small markets and monopoly pricing make transnational comparisons important in determining a firm's competitiveness. Make sure profitability is not solely due to government-sanctioned protections.

4. *Staggered loan maturities.* Even the best emerging market company can be caught in a refinancing bind during a sovereign economic crisis. Loan maturities should be staggered, so there's little chance of a major repayment coinciding with a crisis.

5. *Collateral is good.* In the emerging markets, collateral plays a larger role than in the West, due to the weak position of unsecured lenders in Third World legal systems. Lenders should look for security and subsidiary guarantees.

6. *Lend to large borrowers.* Lending to smaller borrowers is riskier than lending to larger ones. Small firms have fewer management resources and less diversification among customers and product lines. Large firms are more likely to acknowledge Western standards of management conduct, responsibility, and information disclosure.

7. *Sound documentation.* A sizeable number of U.S. dollar-denominated loans and bonds have sloppy documentation. In a restructuring situation, this favors the borrower. Lenders should insist on detailed loan documentation, restrictive covenants, and sensible administration.

8. *Exports or export potential.* A hard currency borrower should either export a portion of its product or have the potential to export.

9. *Structured deals and multilateral participation.* Export securitization deals and multilateral syndicated loans offer extra protection.

10. *Margin of safety.* Whatever your lending standards are in the developed world, add a margin of safety for the emerging market credit. Remember the words of a wise old banker, "Any fool can lend money, but it takes a lot of skill to get it back." For 3 percent in extra yield, lenders can't afford to risk 100 percent of principal.

CHAPTER 10

Foreign Lenders and Troubled Borrowers

No institution extends a loan with the expectation that the borrower is not going to pay. In fact, the vast majority of borrowers do not default or restructure their obligations. In the emerging markets, most of the borrowers are considered "junk bond" credits by U.S. dollar lenders, and naturally, the incidence of default or restructuring is much higher than average. Repayment problems reflect the business, currency, and political risks discussed earlier. In this chapter, we cover the difficult environment confronting foreign lenders that have unhealthy borrowers.

TROUBLED COMPANIES DEFINED

Troubled companies in developing nations fit into three profiles:

1. *High leverage.* The company is operationally profitable *before* interest costs, but incurs net losses *after* interest expense is applied. This situation is unsustainable in the long-run. This problem is common in countries that undergo significant devaluations. A local operator initially saves money by incurring U.S. dollar-dominated debts. When the devaluation takes place, the face value of his U.S. dollar debts doubles in local currency terms but his local profits don't increase.

2. *Turnaround.* The company's underlying business is in trouble. It is either losing money or is marginally profitable at the operating level. It needs new management, new product lines, or new capital. In certain cases, old managers are replaced, and the investor bets on a reversal of the trend. Lenders have plenty of warning before a client company falls into this category. Financial reports supplied to the lender every quarter depict a steady deterioration in the accounts, and the borrower usually requests covenant relief before a default takes place.

3. *Transfer victim.* The company generates cash and profits in local terms, but the home country prohibits it from accessing foreign exchange. As a result, the company can't pay debt service to international lenders. (See Table 10.1.)

Most loan agreements and bond indentures restrict the activities of the borrower and require it to maintain specific financial ratios. If poor results cause a borrower to flunk a test, management's first course of action is to ask for a temporary waiver of the covenant until the company's "house is back in order." Assuming the lackluster performance continues, the waiver requests are repeated until the company begins having serious problems (i.e., when principal and interest payments can't be made on a timely basis).

TABLE 10.1   Comparing Problem Companies

High Leverage Company		Turnaround Candidate		Transfer Victim	
Sales	$1,000	Sales	$1,000	Sales	$1,000
EBIT	50	EBIT	(10)	EBIT	50
Interest	(75)	Interest	(15)	Interest	(10)
Pretax Income	(25)	Pretax Income	(25)	Pretax Income	40
The high-leverage problem company loses money after interest expense.		The turnaround company loses money at the operating level.		The transfer victim makes money, but can't exchange it into foreign currency.	

SEQUENCE OF EVENTS FOR A TROUBLED
U.S. BORROWER

When a U.S. borrower indicates that it cannot make an upcoming debt service payment, the lender considers its options. Assuming the business continues to be a viable going concern, lenders to a U.S. company generally ask the company to put itself up for sale, in the anticipation that sale proceeds will cover most of the debt obligations. If management resists this option, the compromise course is a negotiated restructuring of the firm's debts. The lenders collectively reduce principal amounts, extend payment terms, and accept a partial ownership interest in return. Getting shareholders and most lenders "on board" for a debt restructuring is a challenging task, and the failure of such discussions in a developed nation like the United States leads to a formal default and bankruptcy.

In the United States and many other Western nations, the bankrupt debtor is placed under the jurisdiction of a judge, who administers the debtor's business as its various constituents try to agree on a court-certified restructuring plan that obligates all parties. During the workout process, the same management team that led the company into bankruptcy is usually running the day-to-day operations, and asking the judge for guidance on strategic corporate actions. Depending on the strength of the underlying business, the company is eventually reorganized or sold, and the lenders escape with a partial recovery of their loans. With little seniority in a legal sense, stockholders end up with an ownership interest ranging from zero to 10 percent in the reformulated debtor. Lenders take a 20 percent to 50 percent "haircut" on their loans and receive a majority equity interest. For companies at the $50 million to $1 billion level, the bankruptcy cycle extends from two to four years, although prepackaged versions shorten the time period to as little as six months (see Table 10.2).

The "stick" that the lenders hold over the head of the U.S. borrower is the threat of a forced bankruptcy and a court-administered reorganization. This scenario is almost guaranteed to wipe out

TABLE 10.2 Steps for a Lender to Take When a Borrower Can't Pay Debt Service

Action in the United States	Emerging Market Comparison
Step 1: *Sell the company*	
Lenders usually urge shareholders to sell the company. A better-capitalized firm, with skillful management, is capable of turning around the borrower. Sale proceeds are provided to lenders.	Family owners of an emerging market business flatly refuse to sell. The business has been in family hands for generations. No foreign lender will force a sale.
Step 2: *Restructure debts, give up partial ownership*	
In return for taking a loss on principal and extending payment terms, U.S. lenders demand common stock and warrants in the restructured enterprise. Without a fair deal, lenders threaten bankruptcy, where owners could receive next to nothing.	Emerging market stockholders seek a reduction of debt principal and extended terms—*without* providing an ownership interest to lenders in return. Families are loathe to dilute their ownership and accept foreign shareholders. Meanwhile, local lenders resist principal reduction and equity swaps, because they can't afford to book the losses.
Step 3: *If steps 1 and 2 fail, lender can force a bankruptcy*	
Bankruptcy proceedings in the United States are time consuming and expensive. Management is poorly motivated and the debtor's estate value diminishes.	Emerging market local owners realize that foreign lenders are uneasy about the uncertain outcome of bankruptcy proceedings in a developing country. Few emerging market borrowers were placed into bankruptcy by foreign lenders in the 1990s, despite multiple economic crises. This situation provides undue leverage to borrowers in steps 1 and 2, at the expense of lenders.

equity value, so stockholders have an incentive to cooperate with lenders and avoid a bankruptcy filing.

Lenders prefer to avoid bankruptcy court, but they're reasonably confident on outcomes. Bankruptcy courts in the United States have extensive experience in reorganizing debtors and they follow precedents set by previous cases. This adherence to precedent enables distressed securities investors to take major positions in the debt of bankrupt companies, with a calculated assurance of how the reorganization process will unfold. This confidence level shows in the narrow trading ranges of many defaulted bonds, the prices of which are less volatile than most high-tech stocks.

CONTRASTING SITUATION FOR AN EMERGING MARKET BORROWER

In contrast, the bankruptcy process in the emerging markets is fraught with delay, uncertainty and risk from the foreign lender's point of view. Timing is a problem. Most of the developing countries have no formal bankruptcy courts, so the judges overseeing the cases are generalists, and they're not used to the complexity of such cases. Simply getting a jurist up-to-speed on the intricacies of a sizeable bankruptcy takes time, and the creditors compete with a court docket that is crowded to begin with. Furthermore, the administrative workload of a distressed situation—with its multiple classes of creditors, thousands of claims, and flurry of lawsuits—can overwhelm the back office of a judicial system. Supporting a lengthy case is the family that controls the debtor. The family is cognizant of the foreigners' desire to settle matters and move on. To frustrate the foreign lenders, the stockholders apply any number of delaying tactics. The end result is a reorganization process that can drag on for 5 to 10 years.

The uncertain outcome of an emerging market bankruptcy is problematic for foreign lenders. Like other commercial laws in these countries, bankruptcy statutes tend to be vague, and the lack of judicial or legislative guidance allows broad discretion on the part of government authorities implementing the laws. Even when the solvency codes are clear, "they don't have any teeth," says Robert Caldwell, an attorney with Clifford Chance in Hong Kong. This produces legal uncertainties, even when the judges apply the laws fairly to both locals and foreigners. In the countries using civil law or the Napoleonic code, judges are not bound by precedent in making rulings, leaving the door open to arbitrary rulings that may seem inequitable to lenders. Realistically, practical workout experience is limited in these nations. The cozy interrelationships between large operating firms and the home country financiers keep complex bankruptcies to a minimum, so any foreign lender that wants to "pull the plug" on a recalcitrant borrower makes a speculative bet on what his recovery will be.

A bankruptcy allows the existing management to continue running the business for years. This causes real headaches for the lenders, suggests Bob Schmitz, a Singapore-based investment banker, "Operators can really hide cash from lenders in a distressed situation, and I haven't seen a 'sweep' mechanism yet that effectively prevents it." The result of a bankruptcy for lenders is then problematic. The management can bleed cash out of the enterprise for the 5 to 10 years needed to restructure, leaving the company worth far less than when the insolvency started.

Outside of the legal niceties is the perception, discussed earlier in the book, that foreigners don't receive equal treatment compared to the home country borrower. Local judges are open to pressure from influential families, or money secretly changes hands to promote the interests of one side over another. The lack of major corporate bankruptcies in the Third World—and subsequent court-ordered restructurings—prevents an actual proof of this hypothesis, but international bond portfolio managers are quick to point out specific instances of unfairness in the few workout situations that make headlines.

For example, foreign lenders complained loudly about the preferential treatment given South Korean banks in the Daewoo restructuring. In Mexico, when the GMD conglomerate had financial problems, it sold assets to pay off Mexican creditors, while leaving foreign bondholders in the cold. Alliance Capital filed suit to ask that asset sale proceeds be allocated equally, and lost the case. In China, GITIC, a diversified investment company, defaulted on hundreds of millions of loans. Local investors got paid-out first from corporate asset liquidations. When foreign bondholders attempted to collect on guaranties, their efforts were thwarted by legal technicalities; the guarantors welched on their obligations.

POOR NEGOTIATING STANCE FOR THE WESTERN LENDERS

Logic, perception, and experience encourage foreign lenders to pursue the negotiated restructuring of a defaulted loan at all costs, and a forced bankruptcy is almost unthinkable. When I worked at the IFC, only a handful of troubled companies—out of dozens of distressed situations—were placed into involuntary bankruptcy. An IFC chief counsel recalled only two liquidations of IFC's loan collateral over a 25-year period. The syndicate banks in IFC's deals adhere to the policy of negotiating with borrowers, rather than foreclosing on them. This position deprives the Western bank of negotiating leverage, and it gives local owners much more power in a workout than is the case in a U.S. setting.

This power manifests itself in several ways. Uniformly, emerging market owners refuse lenders' requests to sell the business when a default appears likely. The owners reason that the company has been in the family for years, they have the right to run the business, and no one—particularly a foreign lender or bondholder—is going to take it away from them. "Asian families cling to their shareholding like grim death," says a local bankruptcy lawyer. The rock-solid stance toward keeping control carries down to restructuring negotiations. When lenders suggest that a voluntary write-down of principal (i.e., lender losses) be exchanged for common stock in the debtor (i.e., which means ownership dilution for the family), the response is negative, and it is accompanied by an inference that the lender's purview should never extend into equity, no matter what the circumstance. Attempts by the lender to find a middle ground for sharing financial setbacks are often fruitless, and the owners, unmoved by minority stockholders who want things to advance, are quite content to forestall corporate progress in the quest to maintain their controlling interest. If both sides remain recalcitrant, nothing happens to resolve the problem. (See Table 10.2.)

Complicating the foreign lenders' situation is the reluctance of local banks to cooperate in a conventional restructuring. Many are undercapitalized and can ill afford a book loss from writing down a borrower's loan. At this writing, nonperforming loans are five times loan-loss provisions in Indonesia, Korea, Malaysia, Thailand, and China. "The average bank wants to put a restructuring off and hopes the borrower's problems go away when the economy gets better," suggests Algun Branigan, an investment banker with Dresdner Kleinwort Benson in Bangkok. "The equity portion of a restructuring is poorly understood by local lenders," says another workout expert, "and it's hard to value." Among Western institutions, Japanese banks stand out for their reluctance to take book losses, and this attitude slows Asian restructurings.

In the unusual case where a U.S.-style restructuring is accomplished, the lenders' poor negotiating stance is demonstrated. Altos Hornos de Mexico, S.A., the Mexican steelmaker, was technically insolvent in 1998, and suspended payments on $1.85 billion in debt. After two years of negotiations, the Western banks forgave $500 million in principal for an equity interest valued at $100 million, indicating an 80 percent haircut. The prominent Ancira and Autrey families, who owned 87 percent of the business prior to the restructuring, ended up with a 47 percent ownership after the banks' write down. In contrast, the owners of a similar distressed property in the United States would have escaped with at most a 2 percent to 5 percent stake.

PT Argo Pantes, the Indonesian textile maker, was technically insolvent in 1997, and suspended payments on $189 million in unsecured debt. After three and one-half years of negotiations, the Western banks agreed to forgive $125 million in principal for a maximum 70 percent equity interest, indicating a 66 percent haircut. The prominent Wah family, which owned 87 percent of the business prior to the restructuring, ended up with a minimum 26 percent ownership after the banks' write down, and possibly more if results improve.

Generally, when the emerging market operation is paying interest (but delaying principal), bank lenders avoid write-downs and bondholders provide waivers. With little pressure to pay down principal, the owners dig-in on their refusal to give-up equity. A stalemate then ensues and the borrower stagnates. Practitioners refer to these firms as the "walking wounded."

ASIAN RESTRUCTURING

Three years after the Asian crises, hundreds of emerging market firms fit this characterization. A list of business news stories (as of November 2000) show dozens of Indonesian, Malaysian, Thai, and Korean companies still working on restructuring plans for foreign debts. For example, in Malaysia, Technology Resources Industries, the mobile phone operator, was finalizing another restructuring scheme for its $375 million euro-convertible bond due 2004. Hyundai Engineering & Construction (Korea) was floating yet another plan to repay its U.S. dollar creditors. TPI Polene, the Thai conglomerate with over $1 billion in debts, had acquiesced to creditors' demands for new management—after three years—but the company's obligations were not reduced, leaving TPI technically insolvent. A World Bank study (May 2000) concluded that less than one-half of defaulted Asian firms had restructured their debts, leaving them in financial limbo.

This slow motion surprised Steven Wood, a distressed debt trader at SF Sentry, a California hedge fund. "I left the firm in 1998 to pursue other interests. When I returned two years later, nothing had changed with these problem borrowers."

Most of the restructurings I observed in Asia over the 1998–2000 period were simple reschedulings. Debtors extended three-year loans, for example, into seven-year loans, and received a higher interest rate. A number of the healthier companies, under pressure from creditors, obtained private equity capital, a portion of which was allocated to debt service. The new capital strengthened the balance sheet, but it reduced family ownership.

Positive activity depends on management. If management recognizes the debt load as a continuing burden, it can remedy the situation within a reasonable time period. An increasingly popular option is buying back foreign debts at a fraction of par value, as some lenders throw in the towel at ever seeing 100 percent of principal. Private Indonesian firms are now offering 25 cents to 30 cents on the dollar, for example. Owners draw down cash from their personal reserves (in Switzerland or Singapore) or find third party investors to finance the purchases. In addition to partial cash payments, lenders sometimes receive stock options that the owners can repurchase if certain milestones are achieved. Unfortunately, while growing, these enlightened tactics are not broadly accepted by the local business community. Many Asian owners continue to deny reality, and they wait for Western lenders to surrender unilaterally.

FUTURE DEVELOPMENTS IN DEBT RESTRUCTURING

Stalemates between foreign lenders and local interests do little to stimulate the flow of new investment capital. Policymakers are cognizant of this fact, and some governments are instituting changes to streamline the debt resolution process. In 2000, for example, Srithai Superware completed a prepackaged bankruptcy in six months, a record time in Thailand. Creditors, representing $172 million in debt, swapped most of their loans for equity. Thai Finance Minister Tamin Nimmanahqeminda planned to speed similar debt restructurings by hiring 500 new court officials and retraining 1,200 existing employees. The World Bank and IMF are asking their client states to modernize bankruptcy systems, but to date, progress has been slow. Vested interests, particularly debtors, are satisfied with the current state of affairs, and the developing nations lack the professional staff to set-up Western-style bankruptcy courts.

Under the present situation, there's not much the IMF, G-7 nations, or local governments can do to move things along. They can't force hundreds of owners to restructure their obligations Western-style, nor can they convince thousands of dispersed lenders to capitulate. The passage of time and the prospect of diminishing returns will bring borrowers and lenders to the bargaining table, and they will eventually compromise. As the last few years indicate, closure will involve an extended time period.

SUMMARY

Lending hard currency in the Third World is easy. Forcing an emerging market borrower to repay a loan during hard times is not. Workout situations operate by different rules than in the developed world, and the deck is stacked against the Western lender. Foreign banks and bond funds should be cautious when extending credit for long periods of time.

CHAPTER 11

Latin America

In Chapters 11 to 14, we'll cover Latin America, Asia, Eastern Europe, and Africa as distinct regions within the emerging market universe. Each chapter provides a brief economic profile of a region and offers a few generalizations about the business environment. The comments are not entirely "politically correct," but they reflect the considered views of many Western businessmen doing business there.

Latin America encompasses Mexico, Central America, South America, and the Caribbean islands of Cuba and the Dominican Republic. The region accounts for 7 percent of the Third World's population and 6 percent of its GNP. The countries occupy the middle and high-income rungs of the emerging market ladder, but the per capita statistics are misleading. The region's income disparity is more pronounced than other emerging markets. A handful of elites control vast fortunes, the middle class is relatively small, and the majority of people are poor. Brazil, Mexico, and Argentina are the major economies in Latin America (see Figure 11.1).

CULTURAL ASPECTS

Latin America nations are homogeneous in a number of ways. Spanish is the dominant language, with the principal exception being Brazil where Portuguese is spoken, although Spanish is well understood there. The vast majority of Latins are practicing Catholics, and their principal influence is Spanish culture, owing to the fact that

FIGURE 11.1 All countries south of the United States are emerging markets. The stars indicate non-emerging markets.

Spain had a monopoly in most of the region during the seventeenth and eighteenth centuries. A strong secondary influence is the United States. Latin Americans are heavily exposed to U.S. culture and they often look to the United States for new trends.

From a U.S. perspective, Latin America is the emerging market that is most similar to the United States. The concept of the private sector is firmly established—which is something that cannot be said for Eastern Europe, Africa, and sizeable parts of Asia—and the government bureaucracy and regulation are more friendly to business than other regions. Virtually every high-level Latin executive speaks English, and many have studied in the United States. Almost all visit the U.S. regularly on vacations and business trips, and Florida's Disneyworld is a popular destination for family travel.

BUSINESS INTERACTION

The living environment, architecture, and food of Latin America have a European flavor to varying degrees, and Americans—excepting the language barrier with average workers such as taxi drivers, waiters, and office assistants—should feel reasonably comfortable when traveling to the principal cities. Even though the language is different, many Spanish and Portuguese words share Latin roots with English, and the lettering of the alphabet is identical. Furthermore, though close to 90 percent of the population is *mestizo* (or mixed race), the 10 percent of the population that looks European runs most of the economies and holds most top government jobs. As a result, the American executive deals with a Latin counterpart that looks Caucasian, speaks English, dresses Western, and shares a European, Judeo-Christian background.

Latin businesspeople are generally thought of as less purposeful than their counterparts in Asia and Eastern Europe. This image has translated into the *manana* stereotype, which suggests that Latins pay scant attention to deadlines and are always late for meetings. My direct experience is a diluted version of this accepted notion, and I suggest that Latin executives have a proper balance between family, work, and the good life, which is something workaholic Americans have a hard time understanding.

OTHER ITEMS

The office environment in which the executives operate is a surprise to serious Westerners. Lower level staffers often do a lot of talking, joking, smoking, and web surfing. People appear to be goofing off, and underemployment looks obvious, but the work gets done.

Latin America ranks at the low end of the corruption scale. At the top is Africa, which is in a class by itself, followed by Eastern Europe and Asia. Business transactions involve more legalisms than one sees in the other three regions, but the enforcement mechanism is problematic, as we have discussed earlier in the book.

With a few country-specific exceptions, Latin America's infrastructure—telecommunications, roads, and power—is better than the other regions, but huge groups of people lack basic services such as healthcare and clean water. Ringing many of the large cities are sizeable shantytowns, comprised of tarpaper shacks, wooden lean-tos, and cement block houses (Figure 11.2). Unskilled workers (and their families) leave the farm to find employment in urban centers and they occupy many of these makeshift residences.

EXPORT BASE

Latin America is a major source of natural resources for the developed nations. Mexico and Venezuela are major oil producers, and Brazil, Chile, Peru, and Mexico own important mineral reserves. Complementing these exports is a growing manufacturing base serving foreign markets and captive buyers. NAFTA provided a major impetus to Mexican/U.S. trade, and its principles are expected to be duplicated in future agreements with other Latin nations.

Source: Photri-Microstock.

FIGURE 11.2 The well-to-do live side-by-side with those who struggle to obtain basic needs.

DIRECT INVESTMENT

The region's proximity to the United States and its historical connection to Europe have made it a favorite investment target for multinational corporations. As a result, the obvious opportunities have been picked over by the established players. Alternatives for newcomers are deals that don't attract big Western firms. These investments might involve second-tier family groups, niche markets, small metropolitan areas, and countries other than Brazil, Mexico, and Argentina.

STOCK EXCHANGES

The Argentine, Brazilian, and Mexican stock markets dominate securities trading, and a number of their larger listings operate successful ADR programs in the United States. Most of the other countries operate stock exchanges, but trading volume is light and listings are few. Selected stocks from these secondary markets are available in ADR form.

CHAPTER 12

Asia

A sia is the largest of the developing regions, both in population and GNP. China, with its 1.2 billion population and gradual shift to a capitalist economy, attracts the most attention from the business media, but India (1.0 billion) and Indonesia (200 million) are potentially vast markets. On a per capita basis, the Asian nations fall primarily into the low and lower-middle income categories. Poverty is widespread and quite visible to the Western traveler, as it has migrated from rural areas to the big cities, where most business is conducted.

The Asian emerging markets are a diverse mix of countries, with different religions, languages, and cultures. Broadly speaking, they can be divided into three segments: (1) China and East Asia, (2) the Indian subcontinent, and (3) the Central Asian republics that were formerly part of the Soviet Union. Two notable exclusions are South Korea, which pretty much stands on its own, and Taiwan, which has graduated from developing country status (see Figure 12.1).

The 1997 financial crisis hit hardest the countries that were most integrated with the Western financial system—Indonesia, Philippines, Malaysia, South Korea, and Thailand. With its insular, mixed economy, India was not overly impacted, and the transition economies of China, Vietnam, and the former Soviet Republics did not experience major shocks. The affected economies are still restructuring their financial sectors at this writing, and many of their private corporations are saddled with (1) debts they can't pay and (2) lenders that won't negotiate. The slow progress delays new investment into East Asia, with spillover effects in China.

FIGURE 12.1　In Asia, emerging markets include all countries except Japan, Taiwan, and Singapore (starred).

Most top executives in Asia speak English, but their command of the language (excepting India) is not as good as similarly placed Latins, Eastern Europeans, and Africans. This language barrier, combined with greater geographical distance and drastic time zone differential, means Asian businessmen are not as familiar with the United States as Latin American executives, and they seem to travel less. "The whole business culture of Asia is more insular than other emerging markets," indicates one multinational banker. Moreover, U.S. corporations lack the presence of Japanese and European companies in the region, so Asians don't have a continual ability to interact with Americans.

What the United States sacrifices in on-the-ground presence, however, is made up for in cultural influence. American clothes, movies, television shows, and music are popular, and Asian families send their children to U.S. universities in record numbers, introducing them to American society on a first-hand basis. One example that stands out in my memory is the group of Thai professionals that ran a motorcycle club. Each Saturday, they donned their black leather jackets and dark sunglasses, and motorcycled en masse through the countryside outside of Bangkok, much as Marlon Brando terrorized small-town residents in the movie, *The Wild Ones*.

CHINA AND EAST ASIA

From the U.S. and Western European point of view, China and East Asia are among the most exotic locales. Besides being ten thousand miles and 12 time zones away, the region is home to ancient societies that stand apart from the European tradition. China, for example, was a highly civilized empire when Europe was still in the Dark Ages. Moreover, the East Asians do not look Caucasian; their foods, religions, and architecture are different; and their alphabets, writing styles, and language sounds are unfamiliar. A variety of common European items, like the knife and fork, have little or no emphasis here.

Seasoned globetrotters make adjustments quickly, but the inexperienced Westerner stands out like a sore thumb.

Negotiating Style

Business guides to the region exaggerate the negative impact of Americans' inexperience with East Asia and their consequent lack of cultural sensitivity. The fact is that general business considerations are the same the world over, and the East Asian style, rather than the substance, is something Americans can quickly adapt to. Admittedly, Asian customs and languages take years to learn, but even token efforts by Americans to demonstrate an interest in Asian traditions are worth their weight in gold. For example, Chinese businessmen are highly appreciative of an American's use of chopsticks or his ability to say a few words in Mandarin.

Like any emerging market, China and East Asia require Westerners to have patience and perseverance in order to get a deal done. This involves repeated meetings and social gatherings, some lasting into the wee hours of the morning. A lot of Americans, who want to close a transaction quickly and move onto another assignment, become frustrated at the slow process, but they either must accept the delays, prepare to be taken advantage of, or walk away from the goodwill their initial discussions created.

For their part, the East Asians are highly respectful of U.S. executives, but they are not sure what to expect from the average American. The U.S. executive population is very diverse and exhibits a wider range of behaviors than the typical Japanese or European businessman. As a result, Asians need to acclimate themselves fully to a U.S. partner before moving ahead and want to test that individual at various levels. They consider the extra time to be a worthwhile investment. Little do they know that U.S. executives play "musical jobs," so the person cutting a deal with them today is frequently reassigned tomorrow. Asians often link both a deal and a corporate relationship to an individual, so Western job mobility detracts from getting more business done.

As a rule, Americans start business deals in this area with a naïve approach. They're overly friendly and they expect the other party to automatically respect the rules and regulations of Western business behavior, when it may have never signaled its intention to do so. Furthermore, the East Asian negotiating style is more indirect than that in either Latin America or Eastern Europe, and the related thought process is more Byzantine. Discussions often contain hidden agendas that the Westerner has to struggle with.

The inexperience and impatience that Westerners, particularly Americans, bring to the table works to their detriment. Some Asians are opportunistic about this manner, while a cynical minority are mercenary, viewing Americans as "chickens to be plucked." Having negotiated 100 corporate finance deals around the world, I'd say that East Asians are the best at pretending that they don't want to do a deal, and the Chinese are skillful at implying that "they're doing foreigners a favor by letting them in the Chinese market." To the inexperienced, this stance implies that the Western investor must make additional concessions to move things forward. The tactics seem to work. Surveys indicate that only about one-third of Western investments in China make money.

A favorite tactic of East Asians is to bring up a sore point repeatedly—even if it has been resolved in earlier negotiating sessions. They re-open the point with a claim of previous misunderstanding or a wish for clarification. In either case, by repeatedly saying "No" to rehashing a prior matter, the Westerner gets the impression that he is somehow derailing negotiations, when, in fact, the other side is simply wearing him down into providing yet another concession. As a foreigner, let the Asian negotiators get the issue off their chest, and say you "understand." If the problem persists, my advice is to show a poker face and just repeat the word "No," as I did at least 30 times in a Korean deal. The Korean negotiator always said the company's chairman "insisted on the point" and "it was a deal breaker," but he never walked away from the bargaining table. He was bluffing, pure and simple.

Corporate finance negotiations go much smoother if the East Asian firm is represented by a local investment bank. With some international experience, the banker has a reasonable knowledge of Western financial conventions and smoothes out local anxieties, which are sometimes based on a lack of experience with Western investors. Also, the banker can ask the foreigners questions about their rationale for requesting a specific term; Asian corporate executives are reluctant to do so out of fear of embarrassment or losing face. Resolving misunderstandings early on speeds the process.

The Asian reluctance to ask questions of foreigners was starkly illustrated to me when I taught a corporate finance seminar in Singapore. The attendees were Thai, Filipino, and Indonesian executives. My custom during the delivery of a lecture or a case study was to interrupt occasionally with the comment, "Any questions?" After three days of no questions, I asked an English expatriate who was auditing the course, "what's going on?" "Oh," he said, "East Asians—even executives—are reluctant to ask questions of authority figures—even low-level ones like instructors. They're brought up in authoritarian systems where you don't question your government, your professors, or your corporate bosses." The questioner stands out, and he (or the authority figure) risks losing face in the exchange. The attitude is reminiscent of the Confucian proverb: "The stalk of wheat that sticks up is cut down."

To facilitate negotiations and improve communications in an Asian transaction, practical Westerners retain a local lawyer or banker who (1) knows the local environment, (2) speaks the language, and (3) reads the other side's body movements.

Overseas Chinese

Overseas Chinese control considerable parts of the economies of Indonesia, Philippines, Malaysia, and Thailand, yet they represent less than 5 percent of the population of these countries. Combined with the Taiwanese, this diaspora accounts for a significant portion of foreign direct investment in China, and it is an important economic force there.

Chinese Economic Reform

Beginning in 1979, China gradually enacted a series of reforms designed to place a large portion of the economy into the private sector. According to some estimates, state enterprises now account for 40 percent of production, down from 90 percent two decades ago.

The recent progress is admirable, but China has challenges ahead. Many of the remaining state enterprises are money-losers and owe sizeable debts to local banks, prompting a potential financial problem when the loans come due. Chinese commercial firms often operate in closed markets. Compared to foreign competition, they are inefficient, and policy makers anticipate that these firms will have problems making the grade and paying off debts. The need to prop up the state industries while energizing the private sector is

Source: Dan Habib/Impact Visuals/Picture Quest.

FIGURE 12.2   China's economic reforms are attracting large Western companies like DuPont.

a complex endeavor, and there is uncertainty whether China can pull it off without upheaval.

The under-30 generation in Chinese business is different than the state-oriented management running most of the principal industries. The younger people were never part of the state edifice, and they're more in-tune with commercial enterprise and more likely to pursue entrepreneurial projects. The Southern portion of China near Hong Kong is most advanced in this respect. In this special economic zone, Beijing's socialist policies hold less sway. Entrepreneurs like to mention the Chinese proverb, "the mountains are high, and the emperor is far away," meaning the central government's influence in economic matters is less than dominant there.

INDIA

With a one billion population that is still growing, India is expected to overtake China (1.2 billion) as the world's most populous nation by 2060. With a per capita income of only $370, India is one of the poorest countries in Asia. About one-half of the population lives on less than $1 per day, and perhaps another third affords a minimal lifestyle that includes meager lodgings, a small refrigerator, and a few consumer goods. Only 10 percent to 15 percent of the population have incomes that support basic aspects of the Western "middle class lifestyle."

A prominent feature of Indian society is the caste system, which stratifies the majority Hindu population into four main groupings. Contact between castes is prohibited on the religious grounds that lower castes pollute higher ones. Membership in a caste is inherited from one's parents. Social mobility within the caste system is difficult and lower level castes are consigned to low-prestige, low-paying occupations. From a strict legal point of view, discrimination based on caste is illegal, but prejudice remains strong, ultimately reinforcing the system.

Self-Sufficiency

Through the 1980s, India operated a self-sufficient economy where trade with developed countries did not play a major role. To a greater degree than other developing nations, the state owned key industries, and private oligopolies dominated other important sectors. The lack of foreign participation deprived India of technological advances, investment capital, and incentives to improve quality and efficiency.

Recent Developments

In 1991, the government started to reform the economic system, and a lot of progress was made in boosting the growth rate and stimulating foreign interest. However, like China, India is a difficult place for Westerners to invest for the long-term. The liberalization process is slow, and it is not fully accepted. As a result, multinationals proposing a project are sometimes caught in the crossfire of political argument and government infighting, and the deal doesn't get done.

The tenacity of the Indian government bureaucracy is legendary, and foreign firms (as well as local enterprises) are subject to a bewildering maze of licenses, taxes, controls, and procedures. Compounding this problem is the attitude among bureaucrats that "foreigners shouldn't make too much money in India," so rules and regulations are sometimes adjusted on a transactional basis, depriving multinationals of appropriate rates of return.

Even with these handicaps, India's economy shows steady, if unspectacular, growth and possesses a diversified industrial base. Sectors experiencing rapid advancement are infrastructure, especially power and telecommunications, and high technology.

Perhaps the brightest light in the economy now is the IT services market, which has been growing in excess of 25 percent annually. "With the latest advances in telecommunications, professionals in India can provide managed software solutions to customers around the world," says Bill Pearce, Director of AIG Asian Infrastructure Fund, a private equity partnership that invests in India. "The high skill level of India's IT staffers and their lower wage base makes Indian offshore consulting an attractive option for multinationals." The cost-effectiveness of India's IT sector draws foreign investment interest. "We're actively looking at establishing an Indian subsidiary to handle system maintenance," adds Kaustubh Phaltankar, Chairman of Netplexus Corporation, which provides Internet security services, "With high speed lines and satellites, this work doesn't have to be done in the United States."

SOUTH KOREA

Despite a population of only 46 million, South Korea has an economy one-third larger than India, reflecting the huge disparity in per capita incomes. South Korea is the most prosperous emerging market in Asia, with an economy based on the Japanese model: large industrial conglomerates (chaebol, in Korean) focused on exports, with economic and industrial policy set by the government.

The *chaebols* include 30 top corporate groups, including Daewoo, Hyundai, Lucky-Goldstar, and Samsung. Dominating the local economy, they import whatever technology they require, then manufacture in South Korea for the domestic market and for export to other countries.

The *chaebol's* undue influence in the economy, and their preferential treatment from government and commercial banks, contributed to Korea's recent problems, and the government has proposed measures to reform these vast empires. Shareholder resistance and massive indebtedness complicate the restructuring process, and progress is slow.

For foreigners, South Korea is the most difficult Asian market in which to establish an investment foothold. The *chaebols* and financial system are highly insular, and the industrial policy borders on xenophobic. Immediately after the 1997 crisis, when equity capital was scarce, entry conditions eased, but bounce-backs in economic growth and rallies in the stock market dulled the business community's interest in foreign partners.

South Koreans are familiar with U.S. culture and business practices. The United States has maintained a military presence in South Korea for over 40 years, and the United States is Korea's largest trading partner. Thousands of Koreans are students at American universities, and a sizeable number of immigrants live in the United States.

STOCK EXCHANGES

The Hong Kong and Mainland China stock exchanges have substantial trading activity, followed by South Korea. Many firms with an East Asian focus also list on the Singapore exchange. Activity on other regional exchanges has slowed considerably since the 1997 crisis.

Asian companies are behind Latin firms in establishing ADRs on the U.S. exchanges. The Hong Kong market attracts many international investors and represents a viable alternative for Southeast Asian issuers.

SUMMARY

Asia's huge population makes it a natural magnet for multinational firms wishing to expand their markets. At the same time, Asian countries are important exporters of commodities and finished products to the West. China and India are opening up their economies, but the pace of change is uneven.

CHAPTER 13

Eastern Europe

Eastern Europe is the nomenclature attached to (1) Russia, (2) the European countries formerly allied with the Soviet Union, (3) the five countries surviving the break-up of the Yugoslav Federation, and (4) Albania. In total, 19 nations are represented, with Russia and Poland having the two largest economies. All of these countries are making the transition from a demand economy to a market system, with varying degrees of success. The process of change is only 12 years old, commencing with the 1989 collapse of communism, and the end results are hard to predict.

From an economic point of view, the countries can be divided into three groupings. The first group comprises the westernmost states of Poland, Czech Republic, Slovak Republic, Hungary and Slovenia, and the Baltic states of Estonia, Latvia, and Lithuania. These nations have the highest per capital incomes in the region, and they are the most closely integrated with Western Europe. In the second group are Albania, Belarus, Ukraine, Moldova, Romania, Bulgaria, and several former members of the Yugoslav Federation (Yugoslavia, Croatia, Bosnia, and Macedonia). These countries are poorer than the first grouping and are behind them in the reform process. Owing to its size and different culture, Russia occupies the third grouping by itself and deserves singular treatment (see Figure 13.1).

FIGURE 13.1 The heavy line separates the emerging markets in Eastern Europe from the developed markets in the West. Greece is the only developed market in Eastern Europe.

FIRST AND SECOND GROUPINGS

In general, the first and second groupings are eager to join the West. Despite 45 years of socialism, the idea of private property is still strong, reflecting a 200-year tradition, but market institutions governing law, corporate governance, and investments are weak, complicating the entry process for foreign business. "Management and institutional skills are centered on production in these countries," says a foreign investor, "multinationals have to upgrade local marketing, legal and finance functions."

Adding to the institutional difficulties is the reticence of business executives and governments to close deals. "They realize they are inexperienced in Western-style transactions and they are fearful of getting ripped off," says Lucja Swiatkowski, an East European business consultant. Increased exposure to Western European, Japanese, and U.S. corporations, however, is educating the principals and accelerating the deal machinery.

Eastern Europeans also have apprehensions about Western motives. For example, the Polish government wanted to sell a 30 percent ownership in a government oil refinery to Texaco. Executives at Texaco insisted on a 51 percent equity stake so they could control the business, change management, and restructure the operations, all in an effort to increase profitability. Polish officials, however, weren't interested in instant profitability. They wanted to know Texaco, to see what Texaco would do with the refinery, and to determine if the government could work with the company. Underlying the government's thinking was the question: "Does Texaco want to exploit Poland or invest in it?"

Governments still run major industries in many of these nations, and they will continue to do so, until the privatization process has run its course. Most parts of the state-owned sectors are inefficient dinosaurs of the communist era. Unsaleable to foreign investors and losing money, these firms have been left on life support to ease countries' unemployment problems.

Many of the large privatized concerns are controlled by the same managers who ran the underlying operations in communist times. Through rigged auctions, these managers gained sizeable ownership stakes for next to nothing, and grew the businesses through acquisitions, joint ventures and additional privatizations. These owners now form the core of the region's economic elite, and they exercise substantial influence in politics and governmental matters. Although it is still evolving, the political/economic model is trending toward the Latin American style, whereby 20 to 30 groups generally run things from behind the scenes.

European Union

Assuming no major set backs, the long-term goal of the countries in the first and second groupings is to join the European Union, an action that will provide substantial economic benefits. This objective has more or less been promised by the West, with the understanding that each Eastern European nation has to make significant reform progress beforehand. Obviously, the more interaction with Western businesses that these countries have, the faster the reform process will unfold.

Business Culture

Americans and Western Europeans feel reasonably at home in much of Eastern Europe. The Eastern Europeans look Caucasian and they dress in Western-style suits and ties. The food and architecture are familiar to Westerners, and certain East European capitals, like Prague, are tourist destinations featuring beautiful buildings and medieval castles.

The abject poverty that one sees in Latin America and Asia is not evident in Eastern Europe, and the infrastructure of phones, roads, and power is often better. Private sector executives tend to be purposeful, serious, and correct. Even the typical office staff appears attentive, and focused on doing its job.

English is spoken by many East Europeans, but the most popular second language is German. Education of the workforce is probably on par or better than Latin America, and the work ethic is improving, as more socialist-trained individuals see the connection between results and rewards. Like most emerging markets, the business world is male-dominated and few women occupy executive positions.

The Eastern European negotiating style is more indirect than the Latin American approach. Behind this facade is apprehension borne of inexperience. The local businessman is trying to figure out the Western corporation, study its motives, and avoid being ripped off.

Corruption

Western businessmen can't imagine the steep levels of corruption in East Europe. The dirty business of bribes and kickbacks seems out of place in a region filled with baroque palaces, quaint concert halls, and cobblestone streets. Unfortunately, the culture of corruption became deeply ingrained under communism. Industrial managers had no concept of fiduciary obligation to their corporations, and stealing from the state seemed to affect no one individual. Skimming revenue, inventory, or services from an employer became the norm in the communist years, and it has held over, even as these firms privatized.

To their detriment, more than a few Western companies have gone into Eastern Europe and supported this system. They entered into shady deals with corrupt government ministries or crooked operators. By completing such transactions without consulting the proper constituencies, such as the local community, the public, or the opposition parties, they gave capitalism a bad name. Upon a change of administration in the respective governments, the legitimacy of these deals can be easily challenged, setting-off alarm bells of political risk and sovereign interference.

RUSSIA

Russia deserves a separate section because it is so different than Eastern Europe. Russia is not part of the European cultural tradition. There was no Renaissance or Reformation in Russia, and the Orthodox church there represents a different brand of Christianity. The extended feudal culture of Russia, combined with its 70 years of totalitarianism, produced a mentality that is different than that of other European nations and more authoritarian. Twelve years after the Soviet Union's break-up, there is no democracy in Russia in the Western sense of the word, and a large portion of the economy that is not in state hands is run by a small group of well-connected oligarchs, who became fabulously wealthy by privatizing government businesses for pennies on the dollar.

The communist system dominated Russia for 70 years—twice as long as its reign in Eastern Europe—and its precepts became more deeply embedded in Russia than in Eastern Europe. As a result, the Russians are unfamiliar with the workings of a market economy, and many of them have a simplistic view of capitalism, saying it is just "everyone grabbing for oneself." The fact that a market economy requires certain rules and regulations is not well understood in Russia, and little progress is being made in adapting regulatory institutions to an effective capitalistic framework. For Western investors, the situation is dicier than in other Eastern European states, and required rates of return are adjusted accordingly.

In terms of population and economic size, Russia dwarfs most Eastern European states. However, GNP growth has been largely negative over the last 10 years, and the country has a large foreign debt burden that contributed to its 1998 default. The attractiveness of the domestic market for foreigners is muted by the lack of consumer demand outside of a few major cities; and, thus, Western investment focuses on exporting natural resources and building selected infrastructure.

One banker I interviewed described Russia's infrastructure as, "an accident waiting to happen." Roads, power, and telecommunications are in poor shape and the country lacks the funds for maintenance and upgrades. Until recently, for example, the power in Vladivostok, a major city, was cut off for several hours per day.

Due to its strategic importance as a major nuclear power, Russia's well-being is of vital interest to the West, and it's hard to imagine the United States and other G-7 nations allowing Russia's economy to freefall to the point of social upheaval. However, Western assistance to date has been disorganized, disjointed, and largely ineffective in setting a platform for sustained economic growth. Consulting advice to the Russians has been provided in a piecemeal fashion by a confusing variety of Western agencies, and the proceeds of IMF and World Bank loans have either been wasted in naïve development schemes, recycled to other foreign lenders, or hijacked outside of the country. The developed world needs to do a better job of assistance over the next 10 years.

SUMMARY

Eastern Europe is a trifurcated market with the Westernmost region advancing rapidly toward participation in the European Union. Russia, the largest nation, has enormous potential, but it hasn't fully evolved into a working market economy.

CHAPTER 14

Africa

Africa is the least understood of the four emerging market regions. Other than as tourists, few Western businessmen visit Africa and the developed world's impression of the continent is beset by negative stereotypes. It is true that Africa is afflicted with more than its share of poverty, political instability, health problems, and natural disasters, but there are pockets of democracy, progress and prosperity that don't make the headlines. The once-popular notion of Africa being a land full of jungles and wild animals is seriously out-of-date. The jungle never covered more than a small percentage of the continent's landmass, and the wild animals that haven't been hunted down are now relegated, for the most part, to game parks and wildlife preserves.

In land area, Africa is the second largest continent behind Asia, and it stretches 5,000 miles north-to-south and 4,600 miles east-to-west. It is over three times the size of the United States, and substantially more diverse. The 750 million people living in its 53 countries speak hundreds of languages, reside in differing climates, and come from a variety of cultural backgrounds (see Figure 14.1).

ECONOMIC OVERVIEW

The excitement over emerging market investing that took place in the early 1990s bypassed Africa. A few intrepid investors, believing

FIGURE 14.1 The African continent is made up entirely of emerging market countries.

bargains in the other developing countries have been tapped out, are taking a second look at the region. In this regard, several equity funds have sprung up to look for deals, and a number of multinationals are putting troops on the ground to scout for opportunities.

What they'll find is that Africa is not inherently poor. It has vast stores of natural resources, including sizeable percentages of the world's gold, diamonds, platinum, phosphates, cobalt, and uranium. Several countries are important oil producers, and the continent's untapped hydroelectric power represents 30 percent of the world's likely supply. Its extensive farmlands are substantially underutilized due to poor management and antiquated cultivation practices, meaning the proper development of the agriculture sector could be of significant interest to multinational companies.

Unfortunately, the process by which foreign firms enter these countries and make use of Africa's attributes is more tedious, frustrating, and time consuming than in Latin America, Asia, or Eastern Europe. As a result, the first instinct of multinational companies is to push for the path of least resistance, and to investigate those competing regions instead of Africa.

The difficulty of doing business in Africa, and the lack of foreign investment, is reflected in the continent's poor economic progress. In the 1960s, when many African countries became independent, their incomes and exports per capita were generally higher than most Asian countries, including several of the Asian "Tigers." However, while Latin America and Asia expanded significantly, Africa went backwards. Per capita incomes, investments, and exports actually declined. Heavy debts, misguided foreign aid schemes, and failed economic policies stymied any reversal of the slide, and most of the countries today remain marginal plays for any serious investor. Indeed, the GNP of the entire continent is less than that of Spain, a nation of only 40 million people.

Because individual country markets are so small in terms of purchasing power, the principal interest of Western investors is to utilize Africa as an export platform, rather than as a new market for sales growth. The bulk of foreign investment is dedicated to the export of either (1) mineral resources such as oil, gold, and diamonds; or (2) agricultural commodities like cocoa, coffee, and tobacco. Manufactured products represent a tiny share of exports, indicating the sorry state of the region's industrial sector.

From a businessman's point of view, there are four Africas:

1. *Northern Africa.* The five Moslem countries bordering the Mediterranean.
2. *Francophone West Africa.* The Western and Central African countries that retain a heavy French influence.
3. *Anglophone Africa.* Countries in Eastern Africa (like Kenya and Uganda) that have English influence, as well as several West African nations (such as Nigeria) that share this heritage.
4. *South Africa.* The nation of South Africa and the surrounding nations connected to its economy.

NORTHERN AFRICA

The five Moslem countries in the northernmost portion of the continent share little politically, economically, or culturally with the rest of Africa (which is often referred to as sub-Saharan Africa or black Africa). In business, Northern Africa is closer to Europe, and key executives are able to converse as near-equals with their European counterparts.

Northern Africa is wealthier than sub-Saharan Africa, and the physical infrastructure of phones, roads, and power is superior. The laws are strong here, and businessmen combine the Moslem and European ways of doing business. Negotiations often proceed in the Mediterranean style, with a lot of arguing and discussion, as issues are constantly closed and reopened.

The investment process for Westerners is more difficult here than in Asia or Latin America. Until recently, the local groups didn't have much interest in foreign investment, and government approvals were slowed by a difficult bureaucracy.

The workforce is well regarded and it has a reputation for learning new skills easily. This adaptability is demonstrated by the success that immigrants from the region have had in obtaining jobs in Western Europe.

Arabic and French are the two main languages, with English being popular in Egypt. Income distribution is skewed, but the large

Source: Photri-Microstock.

FIGURE 14.2 In emerging countries, the old and the new often mingle. In Cairo, the modern roads are shared by old-style and new-style transportation.

shantytowns evident in Latin America, Asia, and sub-Saharan Africa aren't seen here.

Northern Africa lacks the racial discrimination found in Latin America, the caste system in India, and the tribal affiliations in sub-Saharan Africa. Recent social tension is derived from Moslem fundamentalism, which wants these states to administer the population according to strict religious laws.

Egypt, Tunisia, and Morocco have well-established manufacturing bases and a number of strong business groups. Algeria is slowly opening its economy, and Libya maintains an isolationalist posture. Morocco has stated its desire for consideration as a future member of the European Union.

Like most of Africa, these countries have a veneer of democracy with elections and parliaments. Reality, however, remains a one-party system, often headed by a strongman, with limited freedom of expression.

FRANCOPHONE WEST AFRICA

Francophone West Africa is representative of the negative stereotypes that Westerners associate with the continent. Virtually all of the nations in this category are desperately poor, with per capital GNP falling below $500. Economic growth has been flat or negative for the last 20 years, and many countries are afflicted with periodic political instability, civil insurrection, and tribal conflict. Open unemployment is over 20 percent, and a poor institutional framework for commerce puts the majority of business in the informal sector (i.e., the underground economy).

The macroeconomic system is in a shambles. The local currency is managed by France and it is subject to periodic devaluation and inconvertibility. The sovereign government is either officially in default on its loans or technically insolvent. Foreign aid from Western governments and soft loans from multilateral banks constitute a significant portion of hard currency receipts.

Political leadership in this region has been a synonym for kleptocracy, as military rulers, civilian dictatorship, and one-party administrations control what little wealth is created for diversion into the leaders' Swiss bank accounts. This corruption, combined with the overriding political and currency risks, starve the countries of long-term foreign investment, with the exception of cash-commodity plays in natural resources and agriculture.

This region has not fully embraced the techniques of the market economy, and government's influence and ownership remains stronger than in other emerging markets. Local businessmen typically view the government as an enemy rather than a facilitator of progress, due to the propensity of the local bureaucrats to demand bribes and kickbacks for providing permits and licenses. Privatizations occur slowly, and the governments still exercise control over vast swaths of infrastructure, which leads to a lack of new construction or maintenance in key sectors such as telecommunications, railroads, and port facilities.

While Asia, Latin America, and Eastern Europe make positive moves into globalization, this part of Africa remains mired in its old ways, and local business is highly insular. Trade with the developed world—outside of a few oil-producing nations—is a small part of GNP. Trade with African neighbors is an even smaller part of economic activity, owing to road systems that lead to the sea rather than between countries and unofficial trade barriers (like bribes to customs officials) that make the cost of exporting to surrounding nations uneconomical.

These nations are not as industrialized as North Africa, but they have more natural resources. Economic activity is concentrated in agriculture here, and the region has only a few cities exceeding one million population.

Colonization Hangover. European colonization seems to have affected these countries more than other African states. They had a harder time moving out of colonization, achieved independence later, and encountered problems realizing that progress depended entirely on their own will and effort, as opposed to initiatives from others. This situation resulted in European nations (and multilateral banks) still running the countries in an indirect way, and large productive assets—such as mines, oil reserves, rubber farms, and palm oil plantations—are frequently foreign-owned.

A few years ago, the West had big hopes. The region's rulers seemed to understand that democracy was necessary to advance economically, but the West's optimism has proved to be unfounded. The countries remain under the sway of the first generation of post-independence politicians, who let political infighting and old-time tribal loyalties interrupt development. Older politicians stay in office—it's a source of wealth—and receive a lot of pressure from tribal colleagues back in the villages to redistribute income back to the tribe. The latest Western thinking is that the second generation of politicians will be less corrupt and will have the ability to disassociate themselves from their village and tribal ties. This anticipated evolution could provide the basis for sustainable progress for Francophone Africa on a nation-state basis.

Tribalism.   Africa has 2,000 distinct tribes, writes David Lamb in his book, *The Africans* (Vintage Books, 1987), "Each group is protective of its own turf, each shares a cultural affinity and each, in its own way, feels superior to the other." There is little intermarriage between tribes, and those tribal members that move up in the world are supposed to look out for fellow tribesmen, by showing preferences in jobs, business, or politics. Loyalty to the tribe exceeds any allegiance to the nation, making the creation of a national identity difficult for these new countries.

One African friend of mine downplays the differences between tribes. "Members of different tribes socialize with each other and do business together. However, people feel more comfortable with the same tribe." He likened the differences to Polish-Americans preferring to "hang out" with fellow Polish-Americans, or Harvard grads wanting to hire other Harvard grads.

Of course, the most extreme forms of tribalism produce divisive conflicts that erupt into violence and bloodshed. Burundi and Rwanda, two Belgian colonies that became independent in 1962, are the most illustrative. They experienced significant intertribal killings between the Hutus and Tutsi. Hundreds of thousands were killed, and border areas became filled with refugee camps. International groups have been unsuccessful in resolving the problem.

Business Environment.   Unlike much of Asia and Latin America, the typical economy in Francophone Africa is not dominated by a group of 20 or 30 wealthy families. Government has its hands in a lot of businesses (often in partnership with foreigners) and foreigners pull the strings in key industrial sectors behind the scenes. Wealthy Africans not involved directly in government might own one respectable company or profitable plantation, rather than a diversified industrial group. And the size of the elite African-owned operation is much smaller than its Asian or Latin American counterpart. Twenty-five million dollars in sales is considered a big business.

The Francophone African way of doing business is unstructured and informal, and it frustrates Western businessmen. The notion of time, for example, is very elastic. An African executive may agree to meet you at 6 P.M., but more often than not, he'll show up at 9 P.M. or not at all. This behavior is not meant to be offensive to the Westerner, for, in the African's mind, the 6 P.M. appointment wasn't a firm promise to meet you. Rather, he was telling you that you had a good chance to meet at 6 P.M. It is an expression of intent, and if he doesn't show up, he doesn't want the Westerner to be angry. After all, the appointment can be rearranged for another time.

The lack of rigid structure extends to written contracts. "We're a verbal society," says one African, "we don't have a tradition of writing everything down." Western insistence on legal contracts sometimes encounters resistance. The intention of the African executives may be to fulfill their obligations, but they may not want to be held accountable for their own mistakes or shortcomings in a legalistic manner.

Many Westerners find Africans to be less than purposeful. "They're informal about following contracts. They might say 'no problem' about a specific issue, and then fail to meet the conditions," says one multinational executive. Their work ethic is not considered strong by foreigners, and this lack of effort, combined with the sheer institutional difficulties, means "Africa requires three times as much energy to get anything done (versus Asia or Latin America)," according to one European deal maker.

The average businessman wears a suit and tie in a formal meeting with a Westerner, and the local executive speaks French, with some knowledge of English. The Francophone region is focused on Europe more than the United States. American firms have not made a major effort here, and prominent banks such as Chase, Citibank, and Bank of Boston have reduced their presence.

In long-term business propositions such as joint ventures, locals generally perceive Westerners as better partners than other African businesspeople. "The locals don't trust each other," says one banker. This view is gradually changing, suggests one African but, for now, "foreign companies should avoid having two or three local partners in the same deal."

In part, the trading mentality of African executives presents difficulties for multinational investors. A common complaint among Westerners is that local business people lack a long-term vision. "They have a trading mentality. What they can get today is better than what's available tomorrow," according to one U.S. executive, "It interferes with putting together joint ventures and project financings."

Infrastructure varies significantly by country but, in general, the region's infrastructure falls substantially behind Latin America. This sector suffers from severe neglect and moving up the "infrastructure ladder" will require years of investment and sacrifice. From the multinationals' point of view, the poor infrastructure increases the cost of doing business in an already difficult environment.

Unlike many Asian countries, labor is not especially cheap in Francophone Africa. The "formal economy" has adopted the French system, and workers are difficult to fire, are entitled to 5-week vacations, and are accustomed to striking. Local unions are strong and the attitude of labor is tougher than in Asia. The chances of using African labor as a low-cost export resource are therefore diminished.

ANGLOPHONE AFRICA

The principal difference between Francophone Africa and Anglophone Africa is the attitude. The Anglophone Africans have adopted, in their own way, the English way of doing things. While there is corruption, the legal issues are English-based, and negotiations with Anglophone Africans tend to be easier for the Western businessman. The economy is driven more by entrepreneurship than in Francophone Africa, there are more small and medium sized firms in the formal sector, the executives are more driven to set up industrial projects, and the business community is more involved in running the economy.

Fewer tribes exist in Anglophone Africa and tribalism is less evident than in the Francophone region. Although these countries have close ties to England and the Scandinavian nations, they distance themselves more from Europe than the Francophone states do, and they operate more as independent sovereigns.

SOUTH AFRICA

South Africa is a lot more developed than the rest of sub-Saharan Africa. Its economy is more advanced industrially, local businessmen are more sophisticated, and the infrastructure is in better shape. South Africa receives the lion's share of direct foreign investment in Africa and its stock exchange represents over 80 percent of the continent's market capitalization.

With its abundance of mineral resources (such as gold and diamonds), South Africa is an attractive export platform, but the country also has potential as a new market for imported products, due to its relative affluence and 40 million population. Per capita GNP of $3,300 is close to the level of Mexico. By way of illustration, South Africa is one of Coca Cola's top 15 markets.

Like Mexico, the income distribution of South Africa is skewed, and a small group of individuals control most of the wealth. This group is more diversified than the typical Latin American nation, as influence is more widespread than just 20 or 30 families. The key executives in South Africa are mostly white, but blacks are starting to occupy important roles in business.

The work ethic of South African's is considered superior to other sub-Saharan workers, and the early British influence produced an Anglophone temperament that helps business. English is the language for international dealings, as the country looks equally to the United States and Europe for foreign investment and trade.

South Africa has been a democratic society for less than 10 years. The country's majority rule is still establishing itself, and the nation's identity for international business is not entirely set. Political risk measures are low, macroeconomic indicators are stable, and the country is one of the few emerging markets with an investment-grade bond rating. South Africa has a good foundation from which to spur economic development, and time will tell if sustainable growth is achievable.

AFRICAN STOCK EXCHANGES

Africa has 16 stock exchanges with 2,100 public company listings. Over 80 percent of the market capitalization belongs to South Africa, which has a stock market value roughly the size of Belgium. Outside of South Africa, the limited liquidity of African exchanges makes direct investment impractical for the average institutional investor.

A handful of asset managers offer mutual funds specializing in African stocks, and a few South African firms trade as ADRs on Wall Street.

SUMMARY

Africa is a tough place to do business. Outside of a few consumer markets, Westerners' principal interest is exploiting cash commodity plays in the region.

The institutional environment surrounding local commerce makes a profitable entry into African countries a long and tedious endeavor. With minor exceptions, other emerging markets offer better opportunities.

CHAPTER 15

Closing Thoughts on Emerging Markets

The last 10 years have seen a tremendous increase in the amount of attention paid to the emerging markets. Thousands of Western corporations, investment funds, and individuals—including this author—flocked to get a piece of the action, and the ensuing gold rush mentality pushed developing economies forward and spurred their stock markets to new highs. Along with the flurry of action came half-baked theories and research reports on the sector, mostly written by people who lacked practical experience. At the height of the phenomenon, normally risk-averse investors threw billions at joint ventures, project financings, and common stocks in risky, obscure places that few of them had visited previously. Suffice to say, those that got in early did okay because they paid bargain prices. Latecomers invested at higher valuations and they experienced mixed results. A good many suffered losses due to the pricing collapses related to the Tequila crisis (1995), the Asian crisis (1997), and the Russian default (1998).

Despite these setbacks, the Third World remains a subject of intense interest for Western businesses and investors. Faced with mature markets, high costs, and fierce competitors at home, aspiring multinationals see developing countries as vehicles for expansion—particularly those nations with the largest economies. On the revenue side, the developing world offers potentially untapped markets representing 84 percent of the global population. Only a small number of these people can afford Western-style goods, but this affluent minority is increasing. On the production side, poor countries have inexpensive labor and important natural resources, and multinationals can use these attributes in establishing operations that export to the wealthier nations. In the investment arena, portfolio managers perceive emerging markets a category that provides attractively priced growth, countercyclical performance and asset diversification. The evidence behind these justifications is not substantiated, but the emerging market allocation for institutions seems here to stay.

INCREASED RISK

There are a host of opportunities in the emerging markets. Investment bankers, local families, and the governments advertise many of them, but it is not easy for Westerners to make money in these deals. In addition to the same business and financial risks coincident with investment in the developed world, foreigners face uncertainties that have added emphasis in the poor countries, including:

- *Political risk.* Capricious or discriminatory government actions that lessen an investment's value.
- *Macroeconomic risk.* Large, downward fluctuations in a country's economic performance that a Westerner can't reasonably anticipate.
- *Currency risk.* Substantial devaluation of the local currency, and/or blockage of the foreigner's ability to change the currency into U.S. dollars.
- *Information risk.* Includes the necessity to make decisions on less information than is available in the West, as well as the heightened possibility of the information being inaccurate.

We have discussed ways to reduce the uncertainty, but it's difficult to lower the risk to a comparable Western situation. For this reason, Western companies demand higher expected rates of return from their emerging market ventures. To build a factory in China, for example, a U.S. firm needs a return that is 5 percent to 10 percent higher than a comparable project in Germany. Projecting this return from an investment—and achieving it—is not always the same, as developing economies involve wide swings in performance that are difficult to forecast.

DIRECT INVESTMENT

For multinationals seeking to sell into a developing country, entry is not easy. Local businesses are protective of their sales base, and the government cooperates with them through a regime of high tariffs, investment restrictions, and unofficial barriers. Teaming up with prestigious local groups is the preferred path of entry for foreigners, and it involves handing over a portion of the venture to the local partner at sharply discounted terms.

It's easier to begin as either an export-oriented manufacturer or natural resource business. Export-oriented manufacturers don't sell to the local populace; and thus, they represent little threat to the home-country elites. Furthermore, export facilities bring hard currency and sorely needed jobs to these poor nations, while requiring little or no investment from local interests. By way of example, U.S. electronic firms own dozens of factories in the Far East that ship exclusively to North America. In the natural resource sector, companies from the West supply the technology and funding to exploit minerals, forests, and farmlands that would otherwise remain unused, since most developing countries lack enterprises with the scale to construct copper mines, gas pipelines, oil rigs, and similar projects. As long as local constituencies receive a share of the profits, the Third World will work with multinational resource firms.

Direct investment along these lines is up substantially, compared with the fund flows of 10 years ago.

PORTFOLIO INVESTMENT

Foreign portfolio investors are also welcome in the emerging markets. Besides providing needed capital to economies that are short on savings, portfolio investment is attractive to local businessmen. Foreigners who buy publicly-traded shares on an exchange have little say in how a listed operation is run. The family groups that issue such securities gain access to capital and they remain relatively free of interference from outsiders, whose objectives may not reflect those of the family.

Emerging market stock exchanges have over 25,000 listed companies. The vast majority involve small market capitalizations and limited floats, and regulators usually restrict foreign ownership. These factors make substantial commitments by Westerners impractical on most exchanges, and the bulk of portfolio investment is directed at 200 to 300 large capitalization firms concentrated in the top dozen markets. Many of these sizeable companies encourage foreign ownership by listing their shares as depositary receipts in New York. All the filings are completed in English and trading is conducted in US$ rather than the local currency. Before moving ahead, however, keep in mind that emerging market equities are not cheap. At this writing, P/E multiples fall into the 15 to 25× range.

Accompanying the popularity of emerging markets has been the introduction of hundreds of US$ mutual funds focusing on this sector. Asset managers frequently narrow their emphasis to specific regions, countries, or industries.

The pattern of actual trading in emerging markets suggests that traditional stock picking takes a backseat to sovereign concerns. Unlike Western portfolio management, betting on the right country is more important to superior results than buying specific stocks. For those who insist on individual company selection, positive attributes of an emerging market equity include:

- A company that has a cost structure that is competitive with international players.
- A company that has a Western-style management philosophy and pays attention to corporate governance and shareholder value.
- A company that has been privatized and has an ownership and management team divided between locals and multinationals.
- A company that is involved with new technologies, and thus avoids the entrenched practices of established local industries.

FOREIGN LENDERS

Western banks, insurance companies, and debt funds dove headfirst into the emerging markets in the 1990s. Premium interest rates and high fees provided fat profit margins. The financial crises alerted these institutions to the risks, and they've become more circumspect as a result.

Lending "hard currency" to emerging market businesses is the easiest point of entry for Western institutions. Due to a low savings rate and a high devaluation risk, debt capital—denominated in the local currency—is scarce and expensive in developing nations. "Real" interest rates (i.e., after inflation) are often 10 percent to 15 percent, indicating a nominal rate of 20 percent to 30 percent. This is extremely expensive for commercial operations. During good times, Western lenders offer US$ loans at far lower rates (9 percent to 12 percent is not unusual) to blue-chip companies. Given the short-term savings, such firms are hard-pressed to refuse the loans.

The long-term implications of borrowing in U.S. dollars are problematic for the emerging market enterprise. Without a substantial export base, the firm's short-term cost-saving plan backfires when the local currency devalues. The translated expense of servicing foreign debts from local revenues then increases substantially. If the company's debt coverage ratios are thin, borrower and lender face an extended workout negotiation.

The Third World legal environment is protective of local borrowers vis-à-vis foreign lenders. In problem situations, loan recoveries for foreign lenders will be less than in a developed country setting. I recommend a good degree of caution in extending credit, and a key guideline is to ensure the applicant's financial performance and market position are superior to those of a similar Western-based borrower. This tactic provides the lender with the margin-of-safety needed to cushion the loan against the risk.

BUSINESS CULTURE

The business culture of the emerging market is highly insular, and financial dealings are dominated by a small group of prominent families. Getting things done requires more patience than in the West, so as a foreigner, you should listen carefully and be respectful of your emerging market counterpart. Often you won't realize the status of the person you're talking with, and you could be surprised later on. My own experience is instructive. In Jamaica, I once mistook the Minister of Energy for a low-level bank administrator. We laughed about the slight at a later meeting, but I became more deliberate in subsequent travels.

The words of David Gregg, formerly head of the Overseas Private Investment Corporation, are compelling, "Be sensitive to cultural differences, but don't sacrifice your own culture." If you feel uncomfortable bribing someone to promote a deal, for example, go to another government ministry, country, or transaction. Your requirements may find a better fit.

FACING THE CHALLENGE

Business environments in the Third World have striking similarities, but remember that each country has individual traits. Westerners make a big mistake if they assume Latin American countries are identical because they share a Spanish heritage. Investors steer away from certain regions like Africa because of stereotypes, but a rational action is to identify areas that are less troublesome. Ask similar questions of different places, and you may find sectors in a country that fall out of the negative mainstream. John Bray of Control Risk Group summarizes this attitude, "Sure, a country like Pakistan might be in chaos, but the trick for Western investors is to find holes in the chaos."

For the Western company, bank, or investment fund contemplating an entry into the emerging markets, employing managers with the appropriate international background is mandatory. Experience in a specific country under consideration is not absolutely necessary. An executive who has worked in other emerging markets will be effective. He will recognize the business and legal framework and adapt his decisions to the local conditions.

FUTURE PROSPECTS

Over the last 10 years, international businesses diverted substantial resources to the emerging markets. The high level of interest brought prosperity to some countries and contributed to economic dislocations in others. In the early stages, the enthusiasm centered around the belief that many of the emerging markets were moving rapidly to the developed country model. Adding to the excitement was a critical fact: the principal developing nations were experiencing economic growth at a rate two times higher than the First World. The case for venturing out of the United States and Europe seemed like a no-brainer.

This promising investment premise, however, was built on a weak foundation, as illustrated by the serial crises that shook the international financial system. Yes, emerging markets are modernizing their economies and inviting more foreigners, but progress comes in fits and starts, rather than in the measured, stepladder fashion that Westerners prefer. Vested interests, like entrenched oligarchs and corrupt officials, are obstacles to legal reform, and the global financial architecture lacks a mechanism to forestall unexpected currency devaluations and financial panics. Strides are being made, but the race to mirror the wealthy economies is a marathon, not a sprint.

Against this backdrop of mixed messages, you may be wondering whether participating in the emerging markets is worth the effort. Western businesses can operate anywhere in the developed world; why consider the poorer countries with their extra baggage? The answer for multinationals that use emerging markets as export platforms is compelling. The benefits of global access to natural resources and inexpensive labor are substantial, and without them a company might be unable to compete.

For international firms seeking new revenue sources, the response is less certain. Most of these markets are marginal in size—compared to even the smallest Western economies—and the larger ones are tough to break into. Long-term vision must be the guide, yet this advice comes at a time when Western CEOs are under pressure for short-term profit.

Portfolio investors have a dilemma. The growth, diversification, and countercyclical attributes of emerging markets are less robust than anticipated, but the huge gains these indexes sometimes enjoy provide an occasional spark to average performance. The trick to achieving these supernormal gains is timing the larger markets correctly (i.e., buying at the cyclical lows and selling at the cyclical peaks). The vast majority of professionals can't accomplish this task in the developed nations, so it is hard to see how they'll be more successful in countries like Brazil, China, and Russia. Hiring the right staff, picking quality stocks, and holding them for the long-term is a reasonable approach, but the typical Western institution is reluctant to ride out the speculative waves.

Emerging markets play a small—but expanding—role in today's business world, and these regions will continue to offer both promising and risky investments. In comparison to the developed countries, capitalism is played by different rules, and the legal and economic environments are less predictable. Gaining satisfactory results is not easy, so those Westerners who want to take on the challenge should prepare for unconventional paths to success. You now have the tools to size up opportunities in a practical manner. Keep an open mind, and remember a quote from Virgil's *Aeneid*, "Fortune favors the bold."

notes

This book is based, in part, on dozens of interviews. I have not cited these interviews in these notes. Most interviewees that I quote in the text are identified by their real names. Where I relied on quotes published by others, sources are noted herein.

Chapter 1

Page 7   Ted Teng quoted in *Wall Street Journal;* page C1, March 22, 2000. "What Happened to Asia's Great Fire Sale" by Robert Frank.

Chapter 2

Page 19   Alan Tonelson quoted in *Washington Post;* page E4, April 18, 2000. "99 Trade Gap Hit Record $271 Billion" by John Burgess.

Page 26   Mateo Budinich quoted in *Washington Post;* page A14, February 2, 2000. "Ambassadors in Latin America"

Page 35   Roberto Cibrian-Campay quoted in *Latin Finance;* page 19, February 2000. "U.S. Investors Spin the Latin Web"

Chapter 3

Page 44   Taber Gargour quoted in *Wall Street Journal;* page A16, February 16, 1999. "Is Egypt Backing Away from Economic Reform?"

Chapter 4

Page 68   Susan Segal quoted in *Latin Finance;* page 22, February
           2000. "U.S. Investors Spin the Latin Web"

Chapter 6

Page 94   Dong Tao quoted in *Washington Post;* page A4, May 25,
           2000. "Acceptance Doesn't Mean Compliance" by Clay
           Chandler.
Page 99   For more information on the multinational survey, see
           "The Intelligence Gap," a Spring 1999 publication of
           Merchant International Group.
Page 101   Jean Marie Eveillard quoted in *Emerging Markets Week,*
           June 19, 2000.
Page 104   Hudson Thornber quoted in *Wall Street Journal;* page
           A17, July 5, 2000. "Corruption Stunts Growth in Ex-So-
           viet States" by Hugh Pope.
Page 109   Arminio Fraga quoted in *Wall Street Journal;* page 20,
           June 2, 2000. "Real Treatment: Brazil's Big Gamble on
           Fraga Pays Off in a Rapid Recovery" by Peter Fritsch.
Page 118   Tom Rawski, quoted in *Wall Street Journal;* page A22,
           May 31, 2000. "China Fiscal Health is Slippery Subject"
           by Ian Johnson.

Chapter 7

Page 151   Mark Mobius quote taken from his book "Mobius on
           Emerging Markets" (Financial Times Prentice Hall Pub-
           lishing, 1996).

Chapter 9

Page 183   Bill Chambers quote taken from his article, "Understand-
           ing Sovereign Risk," from the publication "Global Rat-
           ings Criteria" (Standard & Poor's Corporation, 2000).

index